# Secrets of Empowerment

## – CHARLES GORDON –

FASTPRINT PUBLISHING
PETERBOROUGH, ENGLAND

© Charles Gordon 2010

The right of Charles Gordon to be identified as author of this work has been asserted by him in accordance with the Copyright, designs and Patents act 1988.

All rights reserved. No part of this publication may be reproduced, stored in a retrieval system, or transmitted in any form or by any means, electronically, mechanical, photocopying, recording, or otherwise without either the prior written permission of the publishers or a licence permitting restricted copying in the United Kingdom issued by the Copyright Licence Agency Ltd, 90 Tottenham Court Road London, W1 0LP. This book may not be lent, resold, hired out or otherwise disposed of by way of trade in any form of binding or cover other than that in which it is published, without the prior consent of the publishers.

Cover Design by Mr Kalvadour Peterson
Typeset by Lindsey Quirke


Published by Power Publishing
First Published in Great Britain 2010

# Contents

Biography
Preface

Secret 1.   Is it all a con?
Secret 2.   What is an entrepreneur
Secret 3.   Know yourself and what your limitations are
Secret 4.   Are you an artist or a businessman?
Secret 5.   What is money
Secret 6.   Every time you get it wrong you are one step closer to getting it right
Secret 7.   Focus on being the best
Secret 8.   Setting the stage
Secret 9.   If you let someone kick you in the arse….
Secret 10.  Success or failure is a state of mind
Secret 11.  It only takes a grain of sand to move an Island
Secret 12.  Discipline
Secret 13.  Always express mutual benefits
Secret 14.  Don't hit the first Domino
Secret 15.  Let passion drive you
Secret 16.  Show me your friends and Ill show you your future
Secret 17.  Avoid the unhappy and the unlucky
Secret 18.  Adapt to your environment
Secret 19.  Self awareness
Secret 20.  Walking down a hill
Secret 21.  Interpretation of law
Secret 22.  Language is power
Secret 23.  Qualify your source
Secret 24.  Perfect planning Prevents Piss Poor Performance
Secret 25.  Communication

Secret 26. Who Says crime doesn't pay?
Secret 27. Long term strategy
Secret 28. propaganda and bias
Secret 29. Have a broad understanding of every area
Secret 30. The key is not knowing when to buy but when to sell
Secret 31. Conceal your intentions
Secret 32. Know your worth
Secret 33. Play dumber than your mark
Secret 34. Choose your battles
Secret 35. Organisation and order
Secret 36. No man is an island
Secret 37. Taylor the job to each persons strengths
Secret 38. What is a network
Secret 39. How to lead a team
Secret 40. Reward good behaviour
Secret 41. Objection handling
Secret 42. It's nice to be important, more important to be nice
Secret 43. Customer satisfaction
Secret 44. Be firm but fair
Secret 45. My word is my bond
Secret 46. Aggression and assertiveness
Secret 47. Failure is not an option
Secret 48. Assets and liabilities
Secret 49. Bullshit baffles brains
Secret 50. Money power and respect
Secret 51. The real way to start a business
Secret 52. Man made the money
Secret 53. Self belief
Secret 54. Being content
Secret 55. The con ends here

www.empowermentbook.co.uk

www.twitter.com/charlesgordonuk

# *Biography*

"Life is a stage and the things around us are props. When a person goes into business it can be likened to the performance of their life."

Charles Gordon still recalls his initial reaction when, at the age of 20, his accountant broke the unexpected news: "You're worth a million."

While most young men of his age would have been on the phone to order a case of Cristal Champagne and planning the party of a lifetime, Charles's initial reaction was simply: "What's the next financial milestone?"

While not primarily motivated by the desire to earn large amounts of money, the man with the Midas touch has displayed an uncanny ability to set many a business milestone.

Over the years, Charles Gordon Investments has piloted a variety of successful projects, ranging from lucrative property development companies, to the management and sponsorship of boxers such as Mark Prince and former World Heavyweight Champion Danny Williams.

Ever keen to expand his interests, the entrepreneur now has his vision set on developing a milestone that could net billions--a British urban music empire--with groups such as Big Brovaz and Bootyluv already under his wings.

The irony of Charles Gordon's business life is reflected in his experiences as a child. Although reared in South London, where drug-dealing, robbery and murders have become regular occurrences in recent times, the entrepreneur's story isn't one of rags to riches. His father was a successful businessman, and consequently Charles attended a private acting school, until the trappings of his middle-class upbringing vanished along with the family's wealth.

The entrepreneur admits that his private schooling helped him to acquire the gift of the gab and to develop the poise to interact among the wealthy. He recalls, for example, his English teacher comparing language to currency and power and repeating the quote: "The larger your vocabulary, the more currency you have, and the more currency you have, the more powerful you are."

It was the entrepreneur's exposure to the state schooling system, however, that introduced him as to the realities of survival of the fittest and, of course, the importance of acquiring a measure of street credibility.

In hindsight, Charles Gordon admits that the lessons he has learned from the streets, including how to assess a person's character and being a man of his word, have been invaluable in the boardroom.

"When I was 16, I realised that making wrong judgments about a person and about situations could result in me being killed," recalls the entrepreneur. "The consequences on the street are higher, and so I had to learn quickly."

Charles Gordon believes his ability to survive and flourish against a backdrop of violence and inner city deprivation underscores the fact that there are realistic alternatives, even for the most disadvantaged in society, including Black males. He admits, however, that many are wedged between a rock and a hard place.

Recalling his interaction with the British schooling system, Charles Gordon believes the 'fittest', or those with the potential to become society's future leaders, are singled out at an early age-- not to be encouraged, but to be stifled if their faces don't fit. He remembers a teacher in the secondary school he attended candidly admitting that one of his 'duties' was to "get rid of the leaders so the others would fall into place."

Elaborating on his experiences at school, the businessman believes that certain youngsters are given a figurative cap, labeled 'dumb', to convince them they cannot excel academically. "I was told as a youngster in school that I couldn't do most things, and that I was stupid.

"What is worrying is that if you are from an ethnic minority, possess a strong personality and are outspoken, the establishment views it as their job to break your personality, recondition your mind and send you into society as the puppet they want you to be. It's important for youngsters and their parents to discern and counteract this."

Charles Gordon's pivotal years, like many youths, were those when hormone imbalances kicked in. Life became even more of a bitch when the lippy and outspoken youngster was marched out of the family home after a couple of rounds with his dad, a skillful southpaw.

What followed was a period in a figurative wilderness, drifting from 'boring' college courses to the South London posse culture, and of course from one beautiful woman to the next.

As a virile teenager, Charles Gordon recalls being exposed to women of various sizes, shapes and financial means, giving him the opportunity to be a 'kept' man. But becoming little more than a ponce was never going to be a career option for the businessman, who would often hear the voice of his mother whispering in his ear: "God blesses those who have their own."

Ironically it was the sweet, reassuring messages of the British education system, which labelled him as 'Unemployable', that eventually nudged him into starting his own business.

Charles Gordon is scathing towards the British education system: "I had few choices as a young Black man. I was told that I had no chance of excelling academically and so that wasn't an option in my mind. The next choice was to enter a life of crime, but I thought, 'The odds are stacked against me, and even if I do make money I won't be able to spend the money,' and so I thought, 'What is the point?' The third option was going into business, which is what I did."

Ever since starting his first business venture at the age of 18, the entrepreneur has been guided by one of his most frequently used expressions: 'Work smart, not hard'.

During the economic recession of the early 1990s, rather than go to the local bank for funds, the entrepreneur scoured the property market for a bargain and found a home for £43,000. With the help of a property developer who renovated the house, the young businessman earned a cool £2,000 commission. With the proceeds of his first deal, Gordon bought furniture for a letting office, which he was able to wrangle rent-free for six months.

After launching his first business, a property letting company, his guiding principle of working smart not hard was further applied as he reduced overheads to a minimum, while maximising profits and obtaining a sizeable profit share. He saw the only way to do this was to attract clients by reducing fees to the lowest in the market with a view to establishing long term relationships. This wasn't easy as initially in most deals he was only breaking even or in some cases making a loss. However his objective was to provide an amazing service and establish relationships. After the clients experienced the new level of exceptional service and the relationships were built, he was able to increase fees and move into profits. The clients were happy to pay for the improved service they were receiving. He worked on the philosophy that instead of charging the increased fees his counterparts were charging, he simply charged lower fees with a view to increasing the number of clients; instead of charging one client £1000.00 per deal, he aimed to charged 5 clients £200.00 per deal.

Of course, running a small business at a tender age was a minefield of challenges and dangers. Charles Gordon recalls, for example, how all the equipment in his letting office was stolen after it was burgled shortly after he went into business. He also remembers having to work 24/7 to recoup a large sum of money which was 'borrowed and never returned' by a trusted 'friend', experiencing physical and mental exhaustion in the process.

Charles Gordon says these experiences moulded his attitude to business and money: "When things are going good, that's the easy part of business," he stressed. "But when situations are bad and stacked against you, that is what determines your ultimate success or failure, in my opinion."

After just under a couple of decades' experience in business, what is clear is that the entrepreneur enjoys the fruits of his success. He can often be identified in London by his distinctive numberplates, whizzing around in the most flamboyant sports cars money can buy—a canary yellow Lamborghini, red Ferrari or a black Bentley. And of course, like any young multi-millionaire, he knows how to party with celebrities in tow.

Charles Gordon is now at the stage of life when he feels the need to address the lack of positive role models, particularly among disadvantaged youths living in inner cities.

"For any privilege a person enjoys, I believe something should be given back. I could simply carry on buying more houses and cars and more houses and cars, but that is nonsense," he believes.

"This book will give me the opportunity to help other people to aspire to wealth and power. If I can achieve success, coming from the heart of South London, the reality is most people can with the right focus, determination and attitude."

Charles Gordon believes that Empowerment will appeal to those who prefer to live outside of the figurative box: society's dictates, which are designed to prevent the majority of people enjoying their true potential.

# *Preface*

Charles Gordon: "If you follow the rules of society you will end up with a JOB--Just Over Broke. It's the nature of the beast."

If you enjoy the thrill and challenge of thinking and living outside the mind-numbing figurative box, then Empowerment is the book that will propel you into the big league. For those who lack such boldness, the recommendation is that you shut the pages of this book and choose more mainstream reading, with all its comfortable limitations and normalities.

As the intrepid go through the pages of Empowerment, they will discover a host of priceless principles which have traditionally been hidden by those in power. The result has been that those in the higher income brackets remain at the top, while those with only a few pennies have remained at the bottom of the earnings league, because of not being privy to the secrets of financial success.

What makes Empowerment unique is that it has been compiled by someone who is part of the financial elite, who has tried and tested the formula for financial success, and is willing to 'spill the beans'. In other words, Empowerment is not just theory, written by a university lecturer who drives an Skoda, but by someone who is the 'real deal'.

Empowerment is inspired by the experience of Charles Gordon, one of the UK's most flamboyant multi-millionaires, who made his wealth primarily in property development. In recent times he has successfully ventured into the British Urban music business, and plans to monopolise what he believes has the potential to make him billions.

For the average Joe Bloggs, the book illustrates that even the most disadvantaged can get out of the inner city estates and government funded housing developments to 'make it'; if, of course, there is a plan and a honed mental attitude.

In writing Empowerment, Charles Gordon was motivated by his concern for the youths of the inner cities, many of whom face a bleak future. His message for those considering a career of drugs, guns and shady deals is: "Don't do it." His logic is, why put yourself through a life of hide and seek with the police, burly underworld figures, knives and bullets when you can earn it legitimately, without the grief?

Empowerment is a step-by-step guide on how to earn a good sum by following the simple suggestions of someone who has beaten the system at its own game and earned a load of money by working smart and not hard.

One of the Chapters in Empowerment is 'Are you an artist or businessman?' Similar intriguing chapters, such as 'The Key is Not When to Buy, but When to Sell,' have been grafted into this entrepreneurial bible to motivate and provide the know-how for those who have the ambition to look to the figurative stars.

For the reader of Empowerment the message is: the dregs do not always have to be swallowed, because there is an alternative.

With each key to Empowerment that is used, the fledging entrepreneur will discover he is one step closer to becoming the person he desires, and, of course, richer.

But Empowerment is more than a self-help guide for budding entrepreneurs. It is a stimulating read which contains controversial and thought-provoking views on the British education and legal system, commerce and successful entrepreneurs such as Carl Cushnie. (The first Black entrepreneur to appear in the Sunday Times Rich List).

The book will also challenge the perceptions of the 'street' and the traditional views of those working in the financial institutions around the world, such as the City of London, and Wall Street in New York.

Empowerment teaches: "Arrogance and treachery are crude!" Instead, why not try a more subtle strategy, such as charm, honesty, wit and discipline to win contracts, favour and ultimately power. At the same time, the book projects... fingers up to the system!

Empowerment has a glut of unforgettable metaphors, anecdotes and humor, which makes it a captivating read. The importance of planning, for example, is etched in the pages of Empowerment with quotes such as: "By failing to plan, a person is planning to fail" and "Life is a game of chess, and to be successful one always has to plan five moves ahead."

In countless books on entrepreneurs the Chinese proverb is quoted, that if you feed a man a fish you feed him for the day, but if you teach him how to fish you feed him for a lifetime. Empowerment has been written to put the champagne and caviar on the table; forget the bread and fish!

Throughout the ages, the principles of Empowerment have worked, when applied, to acquire the trappings of luxury--in the first century a chariot or two, a palace, an array of robes, and today the penthouses, yachts, Ferraris and the rest...

# Chapter 1

## IS IT ALL A CON?

C on: to know, to learn, to study carefully, to scan, to pore over
Conman: a swindler, especially one with a persuasive way of talking
Conceal: to hide carefully
Conciliate: to gain the regard of someone or to win them over, e.g. in negotiations
Concoct: to plan, to devise, to make up
Conform: to adapt
Conjure: to practise magical tricks
Consummate: to raise to the highest point
Contrive: to plan

When most people think of this chapter, 'Is It All a Con?', their immediate reaction could be "What the hell does a con have to do with power?" My response is: everything! When you think of the most powerful people on the planet, do they not convince, conspire, and display confidence and conviction with devastating effect? So devastating, in fact, that the majority of their poor victims are oblivious to their tactics until it is too late.

Remember Robert Maxwell, the disgraced media tycoon, whose body was found floating in the sea after siphoning the pension funds of thousands of his employees from the Mirror Group into his private company? It was said of Maxwell that he engaged in deceit by confusion, acquiring tremendous power along the way. For example, he was the only director able to sign cheques, except for very small amounts, and had the entire power of the board delegated to him. To make matters worse, Maxwell always clothed himself with an air of respectability, having the best advisers, accountants and solicitors at his disposal.

In recent times many British politicians have also proved to be bent, after being exposed for ripping off the taxpayer by abusing the parliamentary expenses system, claiming for everything from shifting second homes to toilet seats. Come on!

Believe me, power begins with the con! And don't be confused by some of the lame dictionary definitions that are trotted out. For example, the Cambridge Dictionary defines a con as a trick to get someone's money or make them do what you want, or to make someone believe something false, usually so they will give you their money or possessions.

The problem with some of the definitions just mentioned are that they all have negative connotations, which is part of the conspiracy to prevent the majority from acquiring the very skills that are used so well to cream the system.

One of the objectives of this book is to lay bare some of the tricks of the trade, Empowering the reader in the process. "But", I hear you saying, "this all sounds a trifle naughty, and I don't want to find myself Locked up." Don't worry! The con artist comes in two forms. One of those is the rogue who almost always hides his intentions, because they are always devious, resulting in some poor sod having his pockets emptied.

This book is appealing to the other type, who has all the skills of the former, but uses it for above board enterprises, to outwit his competitors, while fulfilling his dreams and helping those around him.

Interestingly, another definition of the word con from the Collins dictionary is: "to know, to learn and to study carefully". I would add: "Particularly those who make up the establishment, since they often use the best tricks."

Yes, Robert Maxwell's business practises were dubious, but if any young entrepreneur is going to be successful, doesn't he have to concoct some of the principles he used! Consider, for example, the air of respectability that Maxwell always clothed himself in. One of the truisms I like to use when discussing how to take the first steps on the rung to business success is: "Fake it until you make it." Now let me explain what I mean. An aspiring entrepreneur will never fit into the right crowd until he makes it (since he will never have the trappings of success) and he will never make it until he fits in (that is, in the circles of the financial elite). Often the only way around the dilemma is by "faking it until you make it."

One of the secrets repeated on the pages of Empowerment is 'Always give your audience what they expect to see', or, in other words, always fit the bill in the way you dress and speak, the names you drop and the car you drive, if you want to scoop that vital deal, even if it means borrowing the damn items! After all, if you were choosing someone to service a media contract and one prospective supplier turned up in a battered Ford Escort and the other with a dazzling Porche, which one would you choose? Robert Maxwell knew what he was doing when he had the best lawyers, accountants and advisors on his documents.

I know the values we often live by are a mirage contrived by the media, but understanding these values will enable you to avoid being used and to be empowered.

# Chapter 2

## WHAT IS AN ENTREPRENEUR?

" All of us are in the gutter but some of us are looking at the stars."

Oscar Wilde.

There are a rich variety of definitions of what an entrepreneur is. Collins Dictionary defines an entrepreneur as "a person who undertakes an enterprise, especially a commercial one, often at personal financial risk." Interestingly, another definition is "an organiser of entertainment!"

In layman's terms, an entrepreneur can be defined as an individual who has the ability to make a financial dream a reality. All too often, however, entrepreneurs are portrayed as shady characters: wheelers and dealers who are willing to do almost anything to earn a quick buck, even it means selling their mothers.

In reality, the likes of Oprah Winfrey, Bill Gates and Aristotle Onassis are visionaries; individuals with bags of positive energy rather than pessimistic drips!

It's been said that in life there are three types of people: those who wait for things to happen; those who make things happen; and those who exclaim, "What happened?" Entrepreneurs are individuals who make things happen, by working out the feasibility of proposals, implementing a plan and then driving it forward. They are unlike the majority of people who spend their lives talking about what they could and should have done, rather than getting on with it.

The good news for persons lacking that vital spark of enterprise, who have the tendency to wait for things to happen, and who have even exclaimed at some point in their lives: "What happened?" is that entrepreneurs do not possess an instinctive flair to earn money at birth.

Entrepreneurs have cultivated the ability to maintain a burning optimism: the "I can!" spirit. In many respects they are individuals who have avoided being trapped in the web spun by society to prevent all but the elite from becoming intrepid financiers. Some may cry "scare-mongering!" but is it? If the majority of the world's workforce had designs on enterprise, who would perform the mundane, minimum-wage tasks that keep the cogs of the world's unjust economies turning?

The moral of the above story for any would-be entrepreneur is BEWARE! The very institutions that are supposed to help to encourage an individual to reach their financial potential inadvertently lead the masses to a web of financial paralysis.

For example, student loans, credit card debts, and colossal mortgages often ensnare millions in a money trap or web, making the prospect of financial investment too risky. The middle-aged man mortgaged to the hilt will think to himself: "What could I say to my wife, bank manager and children if I invested money in a deal that went horribly wrong?"

To become a successful entrepreneur, an individual often has to avoid thinking inside the box and consequently being trapped financially inside the box--Just Over Broke.

# Chapter 3

## KNOW YOURSELF AND WHAT YOUR LIMITATIONS ARE

Although few of us like to acknowledge our limitations, there are benefits in an entrepreneur accepting that he or she is not a superman or woman.

An awareness of one's limitations provides a unique opportunity to shore up weaknesses, be it in areas such as negotiation skills or motivation, by drafting in skilled expertise.

Simply put, a failure to recognize limitations can be damaging for business development, while possessing a healthy recognition of your restrictions can mean using 'secrets' that empower and will enable an entrepreneur to achieve his objectives.

But there are additional reasons why Empowerment has included a chapter entitled 'Know Yourself and What Your Limitations Are'. For the budding entrepreneur, an awareness of personal strengths and weaknesses will enable him to assess if entering business will likely result in empowerment or disaster!

For example, if you are the type of person who enjoys three weeks' holiday a year, a strict nine-to-five routine, and to switch off completely come Friday evening, the rigours of life as an entrepreneur may not be a wise choice.

At the other extreme, if you are the type of person that is willing to lose family, friends and even your health to achieve financial success, a career as an entrepreneur would be madness. The business world is littered with individuals who in their quest for fame and fortune have burnt themselves out and are still experiencing the tremors today!

Each prospective entrepreneur has to ask himself the questions: "What price am I willing to pay for the loot, and do I have the necessary strength of character to go for the big hit?" If the answers to the above questions are yes, prepare a strategy and make it a good one! History is cluttered with accounts of individuals and even nations who flopped because of under-estimating the enemy, or competitor.

We have all heard the story of how David toppled Goliath, partly because of the size of his head. The lessons that can be drawn from history are that big heads are an easy target for the person keen to rob from the rich to give to the poor. Big heads rarely know their limitations, and there is a saying 'Pride goes before a fall'. An effective antidote for 'big-head' syndrome is the honesty of a trusted business advisor, who will tell you candidly when you are being a fool. The recommendation for persons who want to remain empowered is to surround themselves with honest friends.

The former heavyweight boxing champion Lennox Lewis was known for heading his empire with long-term friends and close family members, rather than a spineless entourage, during his days as a sports personality. The result is that Lennox can now live it large in Jamaica with his loot.

Confidants or advisors can also be used as personal trainers in the field of finance. At times, cosy comfort zones can mistakenly be viewed as limits, which with a bit of encouragement from an advisor can be pushed aside, to experience the power of dizzier heights!

An entrepreneur knowing his worth and potential can also prevent a brilliant idea being binned at its initial stage because of lack of self-belief. In 2003 Jamal Hirani, the chief executive of Tiffinbites, had his business idea spurned by James Caan, the British-Asian entrepreneur from Dragons Den. Five years on, Hirani's idea to provide Indian food for lunch-time workers generates a turnover of £24m annually.

Charles Gordon: "To achieve Empowerment a person must have the right people around them; honest rather than fake people. When persons are not surrounded by honesty they can easily get lost."

# Chapter 4

## ARE YOU AN ARTIST OR A BUSINESS PERSON?

If the average aspiring entrepreneur was asked whether they would prefer to be endowed with the qualities of a businessman or an artist, 99 per cent would probably exclaim: "Businessman, of course!"

In the high-powered world of finance, artistic qualities are considered of little value, while for the artist, possessing any business savvy can be considered blasphemy.

All too often the love affair between the businessman and artist can be summed up in the expression: 'Can't live with them, can't live without them.' But for those who learn to live with their opposite, rich pickings can be enjoyed.

The artist's talents can complement the financial acumen of the businessman, producing an explosive monetary partnership.

Today, we can see how the likes of P.Diddy, the American RnB artist, has combined his talents in singing and producing with an acute entrepreneurial flair. Recent years have seen him produce, amongst other things, clothing ranges and his own scent, which has contributed to his wealth, estimated to be in the region of £188m.

And in Britain the controversial artist Damien Hirst is said to be the most powerful person in the contemporary art world, according to the magazine ArtReview and is worth according to his manager 1bn US dollars.

In reality, few individuals combine the unique talents of a businessman coupled with artistry. All too often in the love affair between art and business the former is unaware of his value in the relationship. This is exemplified in the sports and entertainment industries, in which talented but financially naïve artists have not managed their money well. The experiences of geniuses like Elvis Presley, Muhammad Ali and Joe Lewis demonstrate the point.

If an artist is to cross the bridge and enjoy the financial rewards of his talents, right from the start of a potentially lucrative partnership he has to draft in good financial advisors.

Damian Hirst, is an expert in bridging crossing the bridge between and artist and businessman. In 2006 he invested £15m in his Love of God project, the centre-piece of which was a platinum cast of a human skull encrusted with bling to die for - 8,601 diamonds. The following the his 'master-piece' was sold for £50m by a group of anonymous investors.

Asking yourself the question, "Are you a Businessman or an Artist?" is closely linked with knowing yourself and your limitations. Once you know the answer to these questions, something can be done to strengthen your weaknesses, resulting in empowerment!

# Chapter 5

## *WHAT IS MONEY?*

In his novel, Money, Martin Amis wrote: "Money doesn't mind if we say it's evil, it goes from strength to strength. It's a fiction, an addiction and a tacit conspiracy."

The answer to the question 'What is money?' may appear obvious to many. A superficial answer would obviously be 'a bit of paper and metal that we use to trade or barter'.

But what really is money? What I mean by this question is, what impact will it have on your life when you acquire it and how does it affect society?

For centuries, money has courted controversy. It has been labelled cold, hard, and the root of all evil, as well as the answer to all our problems, and a green god.

Whatever you might think and say about money, it clearly has enormous power to dramatically change your life. It can help to put a smile on a person's face or make a man miserable; humble or bigheaded, a junkie or sober; it all depends on you.

The beauty of money is that by acquiring it you can possess a vast array of opportunities: whether to drive a Lamborghini or

Skoda or whether to eat at top restaurants or fast food; the choice can be yours.

The problem with money is that it can be a double-edged sword, particularly in the possession of the man with two left hands. Yes, it creates choices, but it can also breed limitations. For example, how will you know who are your genuine friends after you have made it? With great difficulty.

By acquiring financial wealth a person can be compared to a yacht loaded with £50 notes, causing every Tom, Dick and Harry to jump on board. For the person who becomes empowered, the challenge will be keeping such people at bay and remembering not to despise them. After all, if the circumstances were reversed it might be you attempting to board.

The moral of the illustration is that with money you may have to offer your privacy on the altar of sacrifice, because of the admiration that is given to finance.

Before you start the game of chase the buck, it is important to acquaint yourself with the rules and rewards of the game. The beauty of money is that by acquiring it you can possess a vast array of opportunities: whether to fly business or economy class, eat at the Ritz Hotel or at the local McDonald's; the choice can be yours. But it has been established that the happiness you experience from money comes from the first few million pounds gained. The £90m difference between £10m and £100m will probably do little to increase your levels of joy.

The advice is: don't get caught up in the game to the point that you lose sight of what is really important and simply chase the buck like a headless chicken.

There are certain riches that money cannot buy. To borrow a phrase from the Beatles: 'Money Can't Buy Me (or You) Love'.

For all my philosophising I would tend to agree with the author and businesswoman Helen Gurley Brown, who is quoted as saying: "Money, if it does not bring you happiness, will at least help you be miserable in comfort."

# Chapter 6

## EVERY TIME YOU GET IT WRONG YOU ARE ONE STEP CLOSER TO GETTING IT RIGHT

Charles Gordon: "The biggest pitfall that many entrepreneurs fall into is being stupid enough not to learn from past mistakes. When trying to establish business ventures, the objective is to turn a negative into a positive."

If one thousand entrepreneurs were interviewed a dominant trait would be their willingness to take risks, even viewing financial losses positively, as stepping stones to getting one step closer to the big financial catch.

The renowned prospector R.U. Darby was said to have stopped drilling for gold after hitting a rock structure which showed evidence of movement, during the gold rush of the 1800s.

Shortly after R.U. Darby sold his machinery, a junkman sought expert advice from a mining engineer before writing off the prospect. He was informed that a gold vein was three feet away from where R.U. Darby stopped drilling. He was one step away from hitting gold! The junkman acquired millions of dollars in gold ore because of seeking expert advice.

The news of the junkman's find could have been enough to drive any balanced entrepreneur to top himself (commit suicide), but rather than give up, he learned from the experience and was often quoted as saying: "I stopped three feet from gold, but I will never stop because people say 'no' when I ask them to buy insurance."

What R.U. Darby lost in gold ore he recouped in insurance sales, becoming one of the few to earn millions from that vocation, back in the day.

Entrepreneur folklore is riddled with anecdotes of fearless individuals who, rather than quit after experiencing failure, displayed a tenacity to fulfill their goals.

Simon Cowell, the music mogul, went through a low patch in the late 1980's when he went bankrupt, losing his house and Porch and moved into his parents home. He also narrowly missed signing the Spice Girls and Take That. Describing his attitude during this period Julie Cowell, Simon's mother said: "I can remember him saying so what I will make it again!"

Today Simon Cowell has made it again and is expected to become Britain's first billion dollar TV man after signing a two year joint deal with Sony, for the X Factor and Britain's Got Talent formats.

The reality of life is that if a person is to become empowered, persistence and patient action is essential.

Soichiro Honda was a master of persistence. The founder of Honda Motors and perfector of the catalytic engine explained to a Michigan graduating class: "To me, success can be achieved only through repeated failure and introspection. In fact, success represents the 1 per cent of your work that results from the 99 per cent that is called failure."

In most cases of success, patient plodding overrides serious limitations in ability, education or resources. Honda developed his automotive company and pioneered major engineering innovations with only eight years of formal education and meagre financial backing.

The message is clear: don't give up, like most people, when you don't see instant results from your efforts. With diligence and patience you will develop qualities that will be rewarded both in satisfaction and in monetary terms.

A slight twist on the chapter's theme is being able to distinguish between healthy and unhealthy persistence: after all, you don't want to be wasting your time and money on a project which no one is interested in except your sweet dear mother. To avoid being led up the garden path always seek informed advice.

# Chapter 7

## FOCUS ON BEING THE BEST

Charles Gordon: "Whenever people ask me why I have been successful in business, I often reply by saying 'It's because I'm not solely focused on making money, but on being the best'."

Have you noticed how difficult it is to clearly focus on two objects at the same time? Try it. The focus on one item has to suffer, unless you are boss-eyed.

Many in business experience a similar dilemma because of having too many focal points. For many the main focus is on making money, and as a result frequently the quality of service can be lost.

Far too many people forget the truism that success produces money rather than money producing success. In fact, in the wrong hands money is a lethal weapon that can explode in your face.

Over and over again, for example, we hear winners of huge amounts of money on the lottery exclaim: "I wish I hadn't won a penny." And I hear you thinking: "Fool. Why didn't you give all your wealth to me!" On other occasions, those who have inherited huge fortunes have ruined their lives because of being addicted to various illegal drugs or booze.

Success, on the other hand, will for a certainty produce money. What is meant by success? Quite simply, striving to be the best.

When an entrepreneur focuses his energies on being the best, his reputation grows, clients will seek out his skills, and business flourishes, resulting in lots of cash rolling in.

Consider Virgin Atlantic. The company's focus is obviously on building a fine reputation, based on a quality service, with attention to detail.

For example, even within economy class, Virgin Atlantic provides a measure of comfort for their customers, in contrast with the majority of airlines, who seem to take delight in seating their customers in cattle class.

Virgin Atlantic's focus on quality has caused its value to mushroom, to the extent that they acquire other routes, such as the one from London to Kingston formerly serviced by Air Jamaica, by saying, in effect: 'We will help you by giving you our reputation.' Richard Branson has made the name Virgin worth a load of money.

The problem with 'Being the Best' is that it goes contrary to the more popular 'get rich quick' mentality. It means always taking pride in the quality of your work, no matter how menial it appears. The result, in time, will be a standard of excellence, because you have invested in time: time to build relationships, and time to learn a craft thoroughly so that you distinguish yourself by providing a service that is just right.

To 'Focus on Being the Best', identify your talents and cultivate them. For example, if you tend to get on well with most people and have the gift of the gab, the field of public relations, law or quite simply an Arthur Daily type-character selling cars may be the craft to choose.

While 'Focusing on Being the Best' obviously requires more effort and time, it is one of the few assets you can completely control. The result over the long term will be a business built on a solid foundation that has the potential to grow.

Conversely, by opting for averages--average product, average service, average qualities--you are saying unintentionally: "Please give me an average return."

The stark reality of economics and the power game is that if you are not striving to be the best in your field of work, what will prevent Joe Bloggs or his mates being used by your potential clients as opposed to yourself?

The problem with the 'get rich quick' syndrome is that it doesn't result in an empire built on a solid foundation. In short, it guarantees that customers/clients will never return to use your service unless there is nobody else available.

# Chapter 8

## SETTING THE STAGE

Life is a stage and the things around us are props. When a person goes into business it is the performance of their life. By creating the appropriate stage in business an entrepreneur will be able to attract and retain a captive audience of potential investors and influential contacts. By failing to set an appropriate stage, your audience will assume the curtain has come down on your business and move on to the next show where there is a bit of razzmatazz.

The above formula may appear simplistic, but would you pay good hard-earned money to watch a show in Theatreland when the written review makes it obvious the play is boring? If there were little or no costumes, appropriate lighting or props, and the script was rubbish, would you waste your time and money viewing such a show, or would you opt for an evening in the pub with the locals?

When an entrepreneur meets with a client to hammer out a business proposal, the review is being read, based on your costume, props and script. The questions being asked by many investors are: "Is this guy's show worthy of my time or money or shall I move on to one with a bit of razz?"

To be successful in business, an entrepreneur cannot underestimate the importance of setting the stage, with the appropriate props. For example, before each business meeting, the question that should be asked is: "What does my potential client expect to see on this stage?" Will they expect to see the props of a figurative Broadway play -- the Lamborghini, diamond bezel watch and a script that reminds them that your associates are in the same income bracket as their own? Or is the client part of the Establishment, who will expect a profile a bit more reserved, because of having the tendency to conclude: "Who is this pimp?"

It's advantageous to remember that each audience that you will perform in front of has different likes, dislikes and aspirations. While a "Broadway" stage may be great for the nine-digit circle (those worth over £100 million), if you are discussing business with those scraping by on little more than a few thousand a year, you could be asking for trouble if you wheel out your most elaborate props and impressive script.

The shrewd entrepreneur anticipates the attitude of his audience before the performance and when in the company of "has beens" and "could have beens", avoids props and the kind of name-dropping that could cause rotten tomatoes and abuse to be volleyed in his direction, during his performance. To use a South London expression, "giving it the big 'un" in front of the wrong audience will not win you any friends, assistance or contracts during your climb to Empowerment.

Rising to the top doesn't always have to be concealment and manipulation. Once the confidence of a client is eventually won, some of your props can be cast aside and replaced with a simple pair of jeans and a T-shirt!

When an entrepreneur knows how to set the stage this can be used to create an illusion of wealth to drum up business during lean spells.

Charles Gordon: "A successful entrepreneurs remembers his unique audience and that he will never get a second chance to make a first impression."

# Chapter 9

## IF YOU LET SOMEONE KICK YOU IN THE ASS, BEND OVER, BECAUSE THEY WILL KEEP KICKING

Charles Gordon: "When a business person has lost respect, it is the beginning of the end."

The moral of this intriguing chapter is that anyone who fails to display a healthy measure of self-respect should be prepared for a good ass-whipping!

The reason for the above statement can be summed up within the saying: 'Give a someone an inch and he will take a yard', or even a 'mile'. Beware!

A successful person is always being monitored, Big Brother-style. For example, if others gauge that you are a heavyweight--a man or woman of principle--their attitude towards you will remain within the boundaries of decent behaviour.

On the other hand, if observers note that you have few principles and are a weakling, they will be willing to rob you and laugh in your face!

A few years ago, a friend of mine related to me a Jamaican proverb, which is very similar to the title of this Chapter: "Slackness breeds liberties." In other words, he was saying that at times we may moan and groan about how others treat us, but often the fault may lie with ourselves. A slack mental attitude may be at the root of many of the problems we experience with others, both in the business arena and privately.

So, while others are continually observing, you must also monitor yourself. With privilege comes responsibility, which you must always strive to live up to. Good leadership is not based on the attitude: "Do what I say and not what I do." Powerful leaders live by example.

To keep the vipers at bay, the empowered individual must make it very clear that they are a man or woman who is willing to live or die for their principles. That doesn't mean you are always willing to go all the way if your toes have been crunched. Below are a few suggestions that will enable successful entrepreneurs to navigate themselves in a dog-eat-dog environment.

To keep a firm grip on power you must maintain a balanced frame of mind and keep in focus that the objective is to succeed and remain empowered. For example, is it worth doing a long stretch in prison because someone ripped you off of a grand or two? Of course not! But all too often a villain will be willing to blow a person away because of a minor diss (disrespect), forgetting his objective. Sheer madness!

Another scenario could be the dilemma of despising an individual who ultimately has the key to a lucrative contract or even two. What should you do? Stick to your principles? In this situation, unless completely necessary, why not send a bottle of champagne or two, rather than cutting your nose off to spite your face?

Never forget that a taste of the sweet life has a way of changing perceptions and making even the vilest of individuals acceptable. Learn the art of diplomacy.

To prevent someone kicking you in the ass, set boundaries which result in some kind of punishment if ignored. Be creative about this--it doesn't always have to involve breaking bones!

Governments use fines, community service or imprisonment, to great success— you can use systems that have similar effects. I can guarantee you it always works. For the bad boys reading this paragraph Empowerment is not endorsing kidnapping!

# Chapter 10

## SUCCESS OR FAILURE IS A STATE OF MIND

If you think you are beaten, you are;
If you think you dare not, you don't.
If you'd like to win, but think you can't,
It's almost a cinch you won't.

If you think you'll lose, you're lost,
For out in the world we find
Success begins with a fellow's will;
It's all in the state of mind.

"If you think you're outclassed, you are;
You've got to think high to rise.
You've got be sure of yourself before
You can ever win a prize.

Life's battles don't always go
To the stronger or faster man;
But soon or late the man who wins
Is the one who thinks he can."

Walter D. Wintle

How true the statement is that battles are lost or won in the mind. You will have noticed, for example, how often the unbeaten boxer performs like an immortal gladiator until his first experience of hitting the canvas unconscious. Often the first defeat in combat is associated with an altered state of consciousness; with symptoms such as doubt, feebleness, and premonitions of another devastating upper-cut.

Throughout the world there are billions of people who are still reeling after experiencing their first figurative blow in life. These knocks can range from growing up in a crime-ridden housing estate to being raised by a single parent, causing many to assume they are being steered to a life of poverty and failure over which they have no control.

I have heard many inner city youths boldly make the statement "It's survival" when choosing to sell rocks (crack cocaine) or some other illegal substance for a big player, as if there were no alternative.

Such a mental outlook borders on the belief of predestination, resulting in the acceptance of life's woes. Conversely, a mind charged with belief and confidence empowers individuals, even those from the most deprived backgrounds, to take control of their lives and steer themselves to success.

When the lives of the financially successful and powerful are analysed, what is apparent is a belief, which provides a springboard for many of their achievements. For example, Reginald Lewis became one of the first African-Americans to buy a billion-dollar company. Yet one of his earliest childhood memories was hearing his grandparents talk of employment discrimination against African-Americans. When asked for his opinion, the bolshy six-year old replied by saying: "Why should white guys have all the fun?"

By the time he reached the age of 44, the entrepreneur, born to a working-class family in Baltimore, won the right to buy Beatrice International Foods, a global conglomerate with 64 companies in 31 countries, for just under $1bn.

It was said that Lewis outbid several multinational companies, advised by a posse of accountants, lawyers and financial advisers, to acquire Beatrice International Foods. Yet the man of humble beginnings had at his disposal 'only' his financial and legal savvy, a recently acquired business partner, and of course a plan and the will to follow this through to completion.

Few individuals are born with such life-altering faith. Most successful individuals will probably admit that, like most of us, they experience the jitters when venturing into virgin territory, but, unlike the crowd, refuse to allow their fears to paralyse their actions.

To cultivate a positive frame of mind that will breed success, make it a habit of trying to chip away at those comfort zones which surround your professional and social life. Not only will a positive frame of mind do wonders for opening doors of opportunity, but it can instil in your financial backers the confidence that you can service that seven figure contract well!

A word of caution for entrepreneurs who have an intrepid frame of mind: boldness in business must be supported by substance. A confident businessman should be able to say to his colleagues during negotiation: "These are the reasons why I can earn us £10m on this deal, these are what the challenges are, and this is how we can overcome them."

Charles Gordon: "Whenever I start a business, I plan it from beginning to end, and in my mind I have already achieved success. I try to cover all the eventualities, all the things that may go right or wrong, and then I'm on to the next chapter. I have discovered that it works."

# Chapter 11

## IT ONLY TAKES A GRAIN OF SAND TO MOVE AN ISLAND

Charles Gordon: "We all have the power to make a change in our lives and the world. When we are aspiring, at times we may think that our dreams are too big to become a reality, but the truth is that nearly everything is possible for those who take control of their lives."

There are a large number of parables that highlight the importance of being aware of your enormous potential. For example, although the mustard seed is considered tiny in size it is often used to illustrate how a small amount of belief can move mountain-like obstacles.

For the purpose of Empowerment I have opted for the title: It Only Takes a Grain of Sand to Move an Island.

Without wanting to appear superior, most people are blissfully ignorant of the potential that surrounds them and within them.

But some people, on reading this book, may say: "You just don't understand my background! I live in the ghetto, dropped out of school at age 10 and was raised by one parent who has more problems than I do!" Others may simply be imprisoned in the nine-to-five rut.

Clearly life does not always present the ideal situations or cards to pursue our dreams. But adversity in life can create the ideal soil to produce an insatiable desire for success.

The Forbes Rich List contains a wealth of individuals from humble beginnings who demonstrate the reality that 'It Only Takes a Grain of Sand to Move an Island.'

Oprah Winfrey, the chat-show host, is often on the Forbes List, but had a very difficult childhood, which included her being molested by more than one of her male relatives. Despite her early abuse, Oprah has become a force within America, was worth a cool $2.7bn in 2009, and was one of Barack Obama's major financial backers for the 2009 American Presidential elections.

America's wealthiest black woman, acknowledges the turning point in her life was when she began living with her father, an entrepreneur, who forced her to read and write a report on a different book each week. He obviously knew that a grain of sand or inspiration can move an island.

The African American woman's experience demonstrates that one way your potential can be transformed into tangible realities is by feeding on the ideas and experiences of successful people, by reading and or striving to meet those who have achieved. The elevated thoughts of great minds can mould and motivate the thoughts of the most entrenched ghetto youth, resulting in actions that can lead to financial empowerment.

Bill Gates is another example of an individual who has demonstrated that a grain of sand, or vision, can move an island. He had dream of having one of his personal computers in every home, in every business and in every school. Today, his revolutionary vision has empowered 1000,s of millions of individuals in business and their personal lives, through the use of his personal computers.

Oprah Winfrey: "My philosophy is that not only are you responsible for your life, but doing the best at this moment puts you at the best place for the next moment."

## Chapter 12

## DISCIPLINE: ESSENTIAL FOR SUCCESS

David Rockefeller, the wealthy American banker, highlighted the value of discipline when in 1915 he said: "Success in business requires training and discipline and hard work. But if you're not frightened by these things, the opportunities are just as great today as they ever were."

For many in society, the 'quick fix' is viewed as the best option, influencing everything from the 'delights' of fast food to the craving for easy money on the streets.

But often, without hard work and discipline, any success can be like a mirage that quickly disappears in a twinkling of an eye. I'm sure we have all had the misfortune of being acquainted with a Mr Know It All, who plays hard, talks fast and has the strut and bucks to match. The only problem is that often his fast car and designer clothes are quickly replaced by a battered Toyota and a dishevelled jogging suit!

Simply put, a lack of discipline and success are not compatible, like oil and water. Have you ever met an individual who experienced long-term success and yet lacked the ability to harness his talents and curb his weaknesses? Unlikely.

It's been said that discipline is something that you must develop within yourself, so you can become the best person you can be, not the one who could have been.

It's well known that successful people exude self-discipline and frequently forge routines that enable them to master their craft, so that it becomes an art form. With this in mind, they vigorously set aside time for their company's development, rather than always being in their business.

If a person is to become empowered, he must appreciate the importance of becoming disciplined in the seemingly small facets of life, such as punctuality and poise, so the pattern will naturally flow into the business arena, resulting in excellence.

For example, rather than being content with a shabby looking home or office, strive to present an appearance that will encourage confidence in those wanting to develop a business relationship with you. And rather than developing the habit to spend profits earned in business, playing the big-shot, cultivate the discipline to reinvest your profits. In the long run, such an approach will reap dividends.

Sky Andrews, one of the few Black football agent's in Britain, believes that balance is required in the area of discipline if it is to contribute to success. He is quoted as saying: "Too much discipline can prevent an entrepreneur being creative and taking risks, while a lack of it can result in disaster. A successful business person has to be somewhere in between."

Charles Gordon: "We all start out with the same alphabet. We are all unique. Talent is not the most important thing; discipline and dedication are."

# Chapter 13

## ALWAYS EXPRESS MUTUAL BENEFITS

"The shortest and best way to make your fortune is to let people see clearly that it is in their interests to promote yours."

Jean de La Bruyere.

One of the first things any successful entrepreneur has to remember when playing ball in the power game is that there is no such thing as a free meal ticket.

For the inexperienced who believe that life owes them a living and that somehow they will get a break from a Good Samaritan: wake up or you may be waiting for an eternity!

Generally people enter business because they want to earn money, and only those who make lots of it may start to give some of their wealth away to charities at the very last throw of the dice. By the way, handing out money for charitable causes is good PR and one way to prevent the taxman from getting his hands on some of your cash.

To conduct business with the major players, an entrepreneur will always be expected to respond favourably to the question: "What are you bringing to my table?"

Those who come to the business table with a begging bowl shouldn't expect any favours. The naive frequently fail to realise that the rich and powerful have their own needs, which usually involve extending the boundaries of their empire.

By displaying empathy and putting yourself in the big man's shoes, one of the foundations of business psychology, a young ambitious whippersnapper can be viewed as more than just a beggar.

Most tycoons are harassed 24/7 by wannabes who bombard them with a hundred and one different proposals that are little more than glorified requests to stick some money into their pockets. For the successful, who have a figurative begging bowl stuck up their noses each day, their likely response will simply be: "Get out of my face! If I give a piece of my pie to every Tom, Dick and Harry, what will be left for me?"

The smart aspiring entrepreneur who eventually wins the hearts and minds of those at the top distinguishes himself from the average entrepreneur by giving the impression that he is appealing to the self-interest of his potential investors, rather than himself.

Attempting to put yourself in the shoes of the wealthy man can be challenging, but by carrying out the necessary research on his character and asking a few piercing questions, a photo-fit of his personality can be built up. For example, does the person have an inflated ego? Is he motivated primarily by money or power? Does he have any competitors that you can help to nudge out of the way? By using the mutual benefits ploy, the figurative stench of a begging bowl--which 99.9 per cent of the time causes potential investors to reel backwards--will be replaced by a bowl with an aroma that attracts others to proposals, with the possibility of investing.

# Chapter 14

## DON'T HIT THE FIRST DOMINO

One of Albert Einstein's many profound theories was the principle of cause and effect, because, to quote the scientist: "God doesn't play dice."

For the purpose of Empowerment, I've decided to re-spin the great scientist's theory and call it the domino effect. The principle of hitting the first symbolic domino, causing all the others to fall down in succession, can be likened to initiating a chain of events, for good or for bad.

To avoid the latter and remain empowered, a successful entrepreneur must protect his weaknesses with all the strength and cunning he can use.

That first metaphoric domino that can harm an entrepreneur could be one of an array of temptations, circumstances or people which could eventually tarnish his or her reputation. (I didn't mention Tiger Woods!) The message is clear: avoid hitting the first domino by avoiding negative people, environments and weaknesses like the plague!

For example, the family of Whitney Houston has repeatedly claimed the influence of her husband Bobby Brown was responsible for the nosedive in the singer's career.

Before hooking up with her hubby, Whitney Houston was a silky-skinned, pearly-toothed, Grammy-winning superstar, who earned a healthy slice of the $410m grossed by the film The Bodyguard. After marrying, the silk skin, pearl teeth and rest went up in a puff of smoke, along with her earning potential.

For Whitney Houston her first domino was marriage!

On a larger scale, British Airways and Air France learned the hard way that safety issues can be like a domino that when hit can quickly have disastrous effects.

Until the Air France Concorde crash in Paris on 25th July 2000, the supersonic plane was statistically the safest passenger plane ever built, with zero crashes and zero fatalities. With a crash and subsequent problems, such as pieces of the plane falling off, it became the most dangerous plane due to its small number of flying hours. With the figurative 'dominoes' falling in quick succession, BA and Air France had to ditch their premier service rather than risk further embarrassing publicity.

Clearly BA and Air France didn't protect Concorde's weaknesses enough!

Of course, the domino effect can also be used in a positive way. When aspiring entrepreneurs strive to give their best in whatever service or product they provide, they are hitting the first domino in a positive way, to eventually acquire empowerment.

## Chapter 15

### *LET PASSION DRIVE YOU*

"Genius is one per cent inspiration, 99 per cent perspiration" – Thomas Edison

'Let Passion Drive You' is a thought-provoking title, which has been used in Empowerment, not because we will be making frequent references to sex, but to highlight the importance of motivation and drive in business.

It's been said that anybody can wish for riches, and most people do. Most of us have friends who are always planning a venture of some kind, but who never convert it into a reality. Only a few accept that a definite plan plus a burning desire for wealth are the only dependable means of accumulating wealth.

To illustrate the importance of passion in any successful endeavour during the 1970s and 1980s in England there was a TV advert for the chocolate brand Milk Tray, with the strap line 'All Because the Lady Loves Milk Tray' (control your imagination!). Those of us in our late 20s onwards can probably remember the scenario. The ad was played out by a James Bond-type character that went through hell and high water to successfully deliver a box of this brand of chocolate because of his passion for a woman.

In business an entrepreneur without passion will not be able to go through hell and high water to deliver what's needed for success. By injecting passion into business a proposal, an entrepreneur will be able to go the extra mile when trying to achieve, increasing the likelihood of success.

Acquiring a burning desire for achievement is not easy, because most of us like to be in a comfort zone. One way this highly charged emotion can be used is by burning bridges behind you, to stir up motivation. To illustrate, the Roman general Julias Caesar, realising his army was greatly outnumbered, concluded the only way the battle could be won was by motivating his soldiers to an extraordinary degree. After his army had sailed to the enemy's land he gave the order for his own ships to be burned. The general then announced: "We win or we die". With the necessary motivation they won.

One way ships or bridges can be burnt today is by having in focus a pioneering ideal that inspires. For example, when Berry Gordy, the founder of the Motown record label, borrowed an $800 loan from his parents in 1959, it was with the goal to produce music using Black artists. It was a vision that drove him in business for nearly three decades, developing one of the most artistically and commercially successful record companies of its era.

When the former boxer and factory worker eventually sold his company in 1988, it was for $60m to MCA and Boston Ventures. Despite the obvious disadvantages and challenges that Berry Gordy faced, his passion for an ideal drove him on.

Far too many would-be entrepreneurs allow the breaks of fear, temporary disappointment or procrastination to imprison them in a rut.

Balance is required, however. There is such a thing as too much emotion, which can blur a person's judgment and even prevent a person listening to advice, since he is convinced his views are correct.

G.W.F Hegel, the German philosopher, is quoted as saying: "Nothing great in the world has ever been accomplished without passion."

# Chapter 16

## SHOW ME YOUR FRIENDS AND I WILL SHOW YOU YOUR FUTURE

(Falstaff From Shakespeare Henry lV Parts 1 and 2 )
All types of contraptions are wheeled out and read in a bid to unravel what the future holds. Curious souls will read the horoscopes, tea leaves, palms or a gleaming crystal ball to discover if they will enjoy a life of wealth and prosperity. But a more logical and reliable gauge in predicting what the future holds is observing or reading the type of companion a person likes to hang with.

Throughout the ages thousands of children have been reared on proverbs extolling the importance of wisely selecting one's associates. Words such as "Show me your friends and I will tell you who you are" are frequently branded into the impressionable minds of young ones by any means necessary -- through consoling words of love at times and, when that fails, by shouting, nagging and a thrashing if need be.

The reason why a person's associates can be likened to a symbolic crystal ball for the future is understood against the backdrop of peer pressure. Even a typical Mr Macho who is aware of the tune he should sing will break out into a cold sweat because of the fear of standing out a like a sore thumb when surrounded by mates who harmonise a different tune.

The problem for the individual who falls prey to the crew mentality or for the clueless soul who has only known crap company is that the song sheet will read something like this: "You may think you're going places but you are heading for the ditch." A person who is blind in knowledge and has failed to select his associates wisely will ultimately end up being lead by the blind, who can only direct him to a future of monotony, confusion, failure and occasionally an untimely death: a literal ditch.

The stakes when selecting friends in life are high, basically success and failure, and so beware. When choosing associates select those who are staring at the stars, rather than the gutter and those who think outside the box, rather than those who may cause you to end up in the box.

It was Mohammed al-Fayed's ability to make friends with the influential that caused him to shrug off his humble background and become one of the wealthiest men in Britain worth £650m. Among the two 'friends' that has helped the businessman's rise has been Adnan Khashoggi, the billionaire arms dealer and the Sultan of Brunei.

When selecting associates try not to allow your heart to rule your head. I know some of your fondest memories may revolve around certain colourful characters who you have known way back when, but if they are going to drag you down rather than lift you up to the stars make changes! I know many a successful entrepreneur who vowed that if they ever made it they would never turn their back on their buddies, but change the tune if necessary. Take a leaf out of the book of President Obama, who distanced himself from his Pastor for 20 years, after his candid views on 9/11 and racism in America threatened his rise to the top!

If it soothes your conscience, you can assist those friends who have the attitude needed to follow the road to Empowerment. As for the rest, you can pop in for a courtesy call during those special occasions, such as weddings and funerals.

Charles Gordon: "If you lie down with dogs you will get flees."

# Chapter 17

## *AVOID UNHAPPY AND UNLUCKY*

Have you ever experienced a rapid mood swing? I'm not suggesting that you suffer from manic depression or bipolar disorder, rather that you have had the misfortune of spending an hour in the company of an unhappy and unlucky (UU) individual.

How can we define the unhappy and unlucky, or UUs? We are not referring to individuals who are struggling with the recent loss of a loved one, or who have just been hit with the news that they are terminally ill, although one might think so.

For the purposes of this book, the unhappy and unlucky may be individuals who are in good health, have a beautiful family, are employed and go on holiday twice a year. They often have so much to live for. But the big problem is that UUs don't recognise this and instead are serially and seriously negative.

We all know the type, and can imagine a common scenario that illustrates their misery. It could be at an occasion which is normally marked by joy and fun, such as a wedding. For the unhappy and unlucky such occasions are ideal opportunities to let rip, be it because of the menu, the quality of the music, the lighting or, of course, the bride's dress.

At this point you may be saying to yourself: why has this topic been slotted into Empowerment? It is because the unhappy and unlucky are NEVER content with making their lives a misery, and consequently you could be in danger. As you observe them, notice the warped joy they experience when feeding off and creating misery in any guise or form.

To become empowered mentally and financially, you must try to avoid the unhappy and unlucky. The reason is because there are two types of people that can influence you. There are persons who nourish and there are those who take delight in draining you or any other sucker they can get their fangs into.

Unfortunately, the UUs do not have a skull and crossbones tattooed on their foreheads, indicating poison, and so to avoid them, a man or woman who wants to progress must be capable of identifying their traits.

When a person is in the company of a UU, an infectious smile eventually turns into a scowl, and slowly but surely one's energy, charisma, self-esteem and, eventually, one's dreams become ashes.

To examine what effect your associates are having on you, occasionally it is good to ask yourself a few pointed questions. Do your friends tear you down or build you up? Do they weaken you and make you dependent on their approval, or do they make you feel strong and capable in their company? Do they make you feel as though life is thrilling and you can climb to dizzy heights with a bit of help, or do they make you feel depressed and void of energy? As you discern the spirit of those around you, display the courage to ditch those who are toxic and embrace those who nourish and cherish you and will help you to reach your goals in life.

A study was conducted on three thousand high achievers from around the world, and the common denominator was not a sky-high intelligence. The study concluded that 85 per cent of them had achieved their goals in life because of their attitude and only 15 per cent of them because of their aptitude.

The moral of the story is to surround yourself with persons who have the right attitude in life. Also limit association with those who share similar character flaws as yourself,(gambling, fighting, womanising!) since this will result in your defects becoming even more entrenched.

Individuals who are UU's can change. Make a decision to focus on what is positive - thoughts, people and projects – to change a negative mindset.

# CHAPTER 18

## ADAPT TO THE ENVIRONMENT

I'm sure we have all heard the saying: "When in Rome do as the Romans do," meaning try to go along with local customs and traditions as much as possible so as not to insult. In other words, adapt to the environment that surrounds you.

In Rome, those who failed to act like the Romans were viewed as outcasts, and although you may be thinking that that was 2,000 years ago and society has moved on since then, has it? Humans still have the tendency to reject those things or people that are viewed as foreign or peculiar to them.

So if you are going to acquire influence, you must realise that you cannot be too different from those who oil the wheels of power, otherwise you will be rejected.

The bottom line is that you must be seen to become part of the family, or at least pretend to! This implies learning how to adapt to different environments like a chameleon. After all, those in power are unlikely to allow you in unless they are convinced of earning money from a partnership with you--the 'I'll scratch your back if you scratch mine' principle.

That's why it is often said that money breeds money, and the same can be true of power.

The more signals you can send indicating 'I'm part of the family', the greater will be the likelihood of you getting that vital bank loan and winning that vital contract. These signals can be many and varied, ranging from a particular dress sense, a manner of speaking, and even the use of a trading name which will be more readily accepted by your prospective clients.

To some people, adapting to the environment may seem like selling out and it might be, if a long-term goal wasn't being hatched. Powerful people have always seen the importance of being diplomatic and able to distinguish between displaying a particular type of behaviour and speech and necessarily believing it.

The over-riding message from 'Adapt to the Environment' is: always be aware of your surroundings, because in the world of business you have to be what people expect of you and fit in.

## Chapter 19

### SELF-AWARENESS

An entrepreneur's self-awareness can be compared to a trump card that is used with devastating effect during a tense card game, to outwit opponents. It means having the insight to know what motivates you in business, as well as the knowledge of what your strengths and weaknesses are.

Each person's motives may be different. For some it may be financial success, family happiness, or fame, while for others it could be the thrill of navigating and completing a new project, or the hope of acquiring a string of beauties to help spend your money.

When skillfully used, self-awareness can help an entrepreneur to clinch deals during decisive negotiations and provide the needed grit to persevere rather than give up when under pressure.

Sky Andrews, the Black football agent, believes his awareness of his reputation as a 'man of his word' has helped him clinch many deals. He said: "I was brought up with morals and I find it helps in business when people are aware you cannot be bought; it distinguishes me and adds strength during negotiation. To date no football player has broken a contract with me."

Many novices in business may be unaware of what their trump card is, and consequently may be oblivious to what makes them tick or motivates them in their field. The result is an entrepreneur who is not able to call on reserves of cunning, strategy, charm, contacts and strength, when hardest hit. An unaware entrepreneur is more likely to be taken out of the game and to fail to become empowered.

Self-awareness isn't only valuable during moments of desperation, but can be used to create a work ethic that is more intense and focused than that of your competitors.

Charles Gordon: "Only when an entrepreneur is aware of the affect he has on people is he in control of the potential reaction and consequently the situation."

## Chapter 20

## WALKING DOWN THE HILL

The hill has always been the ideal vantage point to win a battle. From the hill the enemy's approach can be clearly seen from a distance and the counter-attack launched from the descent and executed with devastating precision.

While an entrepreneur rarely takes up arms to ward off enemies in a business setting -- unless he needs counseling for anger management or is involved in criminal activities -- nonetheless he is involved in a battle. The problem with far too many entrepreneurs is that they are in the land of fairy tales and underestimate just how fierce the battle can become, hence the large number of companies who are forced to stop trading annually.

Once a person enters the battlefield of business, a variety of weapons of destruction wield their influence, ranging from competitors' attempts to entice customers away, changing economies and market tastes, and of course personal limitations. The reassurance is that, just as an army who acquires an overview of an enemy beforehand is likely to be victorious, the same can be true of those engaging in business combat.

By acquiring a figurative bird's eye view on any prospective investment, the discerning entrepreneur will be able to foresee the movements of competitors and markets, before ploughing valuable time and money into a potentially lucrative or loss-making business venture. In brief, such a businessman will be five steps ahead of most of his competitors before he starts to engage in business combat.

To enjoy the benefits of trading from the position of a figurative hill, an entrepreneur must patiently assess matters before going on to devour the spoil. He must strive to forget the notion of earning a quick buck!

Before entering the combat of business, a shrewd entrepreneur will always carry out the necessary research by asking probing questions, such as: How is the market developing? Who are my competitors and how can I out-manoeuvre them? Only by thoroughly carrying out the necessary research will an entrepreneur be able to trade from the vantage point of a figurative hill.

But while patience is essential if a businessperson is to plan from a vantage point, the same is true when he attempts to muscle in on the profits of competitors, hence the Chapter's title, 'Walking Down the Hill'. Don't get me wrong, there are opportunities that come along when an entrepreneur can make a quick financial killing, and of course these should be grabbed with both hands. But frequently success is etched out by planning for the long-haul battle.

For those who have opted to 'Walk Down the Hill', the reassurance is that while they may not necessarily make their first million after 12 months in trading, their business strategy will have momentum. Because the wise entrepreneur has assessed their market, competitors and the health of the economy, their trade will likely be on a roll, and they will resemble the man who is walking down a hill and enjoying the scenery along the way.

Those who fail to 'Walk Down the Hill' because of lacking patience and foresight will pay a heavy price. They can be likened to the beer-bellied geezer panting and sweating to climb a hill, because of struggling to overcome the unexpected challenges of business combat, which he should have foreseen.

Never forget that in any form of business acquiring a bird's eye view of the sector you are entering is essential. But once you have acquired the vantage point avoid running down hill too swiftly to claim your spoil; you may wear yourself out before the battle begins and fail to execute your plan.

Charles Gordon:"A young bull was on top of the hill with his father and shouted: 'Daddy, daddy Let's run down and scr*w one of the cows.' His father responded to him by shouting in disgust: 'Don't be so crude and impatient. Let's walk down and do them all!'

# Chapter 21

## INTERPRETATION OF LAW

Clifton McLeod, the Jamaican entrepreneur: "The law is one of the most powerful forces in society. It is bigger than kings and queens."

Few things are bigger than the law of a country--not the so-called 'biggest' criminals, not the Prime Minister of Great Britain nor the President of the United States of America. Richard Nixon will confirm the truth of this statement.

If you are going to play smart in life you have to recognise the reality of the above statement, and not confront such a beast but work with it.

Never forget it is the law that governs much of our lives and basically runs things.

All too often, however, the average man views the law as a foe. But if you are to become and to remain empowered, due respect has to be granted to the law. It can be a powerful ally or a horrible foe.

"An ally?" some of you may be thinking! "You don't know what I have experienced at the hands of the law!" If your experience with the law has been harassment and beatings from the Police, you may have a warped view of legalities and rightly so.

The message from Empowerment is: grasp the bigger picture. The law in business does not know your colour or social standing, but what it does recognise is money. It can also help to make you more money.

The more money you have, the more protection can be enjoyed from the legal establishment. What else can explain how the wealthiest criminals often successfully evade the law? It is because money talks!

Basically, the law is there to keep up appearances, to maintain a measure of decency and order. When the legal apparatus becomes a foe is when an individual publicly says: "Who are you to tell me what to do?" or when behaviour causes such a public outcry that it shames the law into becoming a foe.

But you may have a slight problem, or should I say a big problem. The majority of the readers of Empowerment have not gone through the years of strenuous training to become a lawyer, barrister or Queen's Counsel. Yes, you can read the law, but there is a huge gulf between reading and interpreting law. The legal system contains an array of subtleties and contradictions which make it very difficult to interpret.

What is the solution? Buy in the services of those who are able to interpret the law for you. The services of a lawyer who can interpret the law are essential if you are to become powerful. Any multi-millionaire will tell you that to be successful it is essential to work within the framework of the legal apparatus.

A good lawyer will not only be able to tell you what the law is but will also be able to use it in your best interests-hence the title of the chapter, 'Interpretation of the Law'.

Can I give you a bit of advice? As you become more powerful, don't be a scrooge and choose rubbish lawyers. Why do you think OJ Simpson employed Johnnie Cochran when he was faced with a murder rap? When trying to solve your business issues, find the best legal minds. No such fortune second time round for the despised ex-American football player, who is currently serving a long sentence after being convicted of crimes, including kidnapping and burglary in 2008. His behaviour caused a public outcry!

For many of the laws that are used to restrict business activities, there are loopholes that can be used to avoid forking out cash. Yes, laws, if used correctly, are like protective forcefields which can be used to protect your interests against enemies. For example, company law can be employed to change the identity of your business interests and keep at a distance those who are after a free meal.

# Chapter 22

## LANGUAGE IS POWER

Charles Gordon: "Language is power. Usually the better an individual's grasp of language, the more currency will be at his disposal, and the more currency you have, the more powerful you are."

Mention individuals such as Barack Obama, Martin Luther King and John F Kennedy and one thing they all had or have in common is their ability to wield power over the masses with the spoken word.

While it may not appear cool to possess a good grasp of grammar in some social circles, it pays healthy dividends in the business world, where the average executive doesn't understand those beloved expressions of the street! A failure to articulate clearly will almost certainly close many financial doors of opportunity.

Empowerment is not saying that there isn't room for street jargon, but that it has to be used in the right environment. In other words, strive to be multi-lingual and to excel in articulation, since it will help you to use the chameleon ploy!

There is a school of thought in business that the less you say, the more in control and powerful you can appear. It's often said that influential people impress and intimidate others by saying less, thereby covering their intentions. However, occasionally playing the talkative fool can achieve the same goal.

For entrepreneurs the power of language can also be demonstrated when setting goals. It's known that those who write down their goals are usually more motivated to reach them! So if it is your dream to earn £2m by 2011, write it down: when you expect to acquire such wealth; what you plan to give in return for this wealth; and your plan for making your dream a reality.

The power of the written word can be amplified by speaking and visualising your plans. Some personal development books encourage reading your goals at least twice daily, once just before dozing off at night and once shortly after arising in the morning. But please, not too loudly and often: your neighbours may become worried and draft in the men with the straitjackets!

Enthusiasm for a plan can be maintained by constantly speaking to a few close friends about your project. But beware: do not reveal too many details about your dream, otherwise your close friend could one day become your wealthy enemy!

Communication doesn't end with what we say, but is also conveyed in the clothing we wear. Our grooming can 'shout' rebellion, wealth, sports, conservatism or taste. John T. Molloy, author of Dress for Success expressed this observation: "The way we dress has a remarkable impact on the people we meet and greatly affects how they treat us."

To avoid being mistreated, it is advisable to consider what is expected of you by the particular social circle you are trying to influence. Will your client expect to see trappings of success, or artistic flair, or could it be wise to leave the diamond-encrusted Rolex and Bentley at home.

There is a clear connection between the world's most famous public speakers, power and wealthy. For example, during January 2008 how much money do you think Tony Blair, the former

British Prime Minister, earned for three speeches in America and Canada, during four days? A cool £500,000. Bill Clinton is also lethal on the lecture circuit and earned £15m in the four years after he left the White House.

Leonardo da Vinci: "Oysters open completely when the moon is full; and when the crab sees one it throws a piece of stone or seaweed into it and the oyster cannot close again so that it serves the crab for meat. Such is the fate of him who opens his mouth too much and thereby puts himself at the mercy of the listener."

# Chapter 23

## QUALIFY YOUR SOURCE OF INFORMATION

One of the first things that the powerful and wealthy realise is they attract speculators like bees to a honey pot.

With financial success, you will inevitably be pursued by like-minded individuals who have heard about your fame and want a piece of the action.

The result will be that a variety of proposals will be thrust in your directions, usually packaged as a 'great deal' that can earn you a bundle, if of course you are willing to invest a handsome sum.

For those who have become empowered it is probably unwise to tar everyone with the same brush and to view such individuals as little more than time-wasters. Remember, you were once hungry for financial success and needed a big break! More importantly, every so often there are individuals and ideas that can provide a quick route to financial elitism.

Joe Lewis the billionaire East End currency trader, made it big by acquiring the knowledge to plunder the overnight currency money markets and by wagering vast amounts on the forward price yen, dollar and mark. On Black Wednesday, 16 September 1992, he was one of the few speculators who bet the pound was overvalued and would fall as the Britain tried to align it with the European currencies. Lewis is thought to have made in the region of $1 billion from his 'bet', and never reveals the source of his specialist knowledge.

But despite the potential to earn huge amounts of money from tip-offs, beware! There are false prophets, the insane and those who would love to see your empire hit the dust.

To protect yourself, always try to qualify your source of information. I admit that it is a phrase that is usually equated with journalists, but for those who are too lazy to dig deep and find out what the real deal is with a proposal, the end result is usually the same--financial loss.

When considering a proposal, qualifying your source of information requires examining a variety of factors. One of the main questions that needs to be answered is: has this individual walked the walk before or is he just talking the talk? What I mean by this is: does he or she have business pedigree?

If you are getting advice from a senior executive who has spearheaded a successful company, for example, there is a strong likelihood that his proposal has substance to it, and that if his advice is applied it will result in you earning a tidy profit.

Conversely, if the proposal is from someone who has never been in business before, the odds against success are obviously going to be greater.

The problem with human nature is that it has a leaning towards gullibility, particularly when it appeals to our greedy nature, so remain focused.

If the person who is recommending a venture is working in a college lecturing on business studies part-time, beware! There is a great likelihood that his business advice doesn't have much substance to it--he is simply talking the talk. Think of it logically: would you be working for a pittance if you didn't have to?

As well as an examination of a business background, look out for other tell-tale signs. What does the physical appearance of the individual convey? Does he have the trappings of success or is his appearance a bit the worse for wear? Are the heals of his shoes severely worn? Shirts frayed? And do his finger nails look like he has been digging for treasure in the dirt?

Complete your assessment by asking a few probing questions, such as: "Where did you get this tip off from and how did you come to your conclusion that I can earn from this?"

To qualify your sources, scrutinise the information you are presented with and the person that is giving it to you.

# Chapter 24

## PERFECT PLANNING PREVENTS PATHETIC PERFORMANCE

"In preparing for battle, I have always found that plans are useless but planning is indispensable."

Dwight Eisenhower

Compared to those who plan ahead, the entrepreneur who is a habitual improviser usually ends up as a pathetic loser with a string of businesses that go down the drain.

A failure to plan can be likened to a football team who are desperately trying to score, but are blind to where the goal is located and are merely running around in circles.

Yes, success and failure in business are intimately linked with the planning process.

The £90,000,000 million question (I love to exaggerate) is: why do many fail to plan? The reasons, or should I say excuses, can be many and varied, but in business there are far too many people who just love to guess or act on opinions rather than acquire the facts; call it an easy-going attitude or sheer laziness.

Ask them questions about their projected profits, overheads, or fluctuations in revenue because of variations in the economy and you will be confronted with a blank stare, followed by a look of confusion and then the inevitable grunt: "Uh?"

For the pathetic that do not perfectly plan, the end result will inevitably be a fall onto their faces and a confrontation with those demons they had hoped to stay one step ahead of: drying-up cash flows, bankruptcy, and auditors banging on the door.

But I hear the embittered entrepreneur who has broken his nose after falling flat on his face screaming: "There is no such thing as perfect planning and nothing that can be done to protect a business when an unexpected bomb drops, be it an economic melt-down or severe staffing issues!"

Of course Empowerment is not saying that there is a perfect plan, but it is a standard that entrepreneurs can attempt to reach before investing their precious time and hard-earned bucks on a project.

The recommendation is: write down what your goals are and when you want to achieve them. By writing down your master plan it will keep you in tune with your goals and how you will achieve them.

A word of caution for all those who are planning to start a new venture: keep your map workable, practical, with careful attention to details, but keep it real! There is an intellectual approach to life and business, which can be a far cry from reality.

To plan perfectly, experience and information are essential, which are not always easy to obtain. The majority of self-made individuals acquire experience and knowledge over a lifetime. For an upstart to acquire similar experience during the planning of a project may require eating humble pie and speaking to those in the know within the sector you hope to break into, to get the low-down.

There are just so many benefits in planning ahead when trying to put together a business venture. Not only does it maintain a high level of focus during the initial stages of setting up, saving time and money, but it also increases productivity and motivation.

# Chapter 25

## COMMUNICATION

Charles Gordon: "Words have different forms of expression in various languages, but a person's body language is always the same and reveals what they are thinking."

You may be asking why Empowerment has decided to devote a chapter to communication, since there is already a section on language. As you read 'Communication' you will discover that it has a broader appeal than 'Language has Power', and, when applied correctly, enables entrepreneurs to enjoy more benefits.

Communication, as opposed to language, has been described as the 'total image'. The reason for this description is because approximately 50 per cent of our messages during negotiations are communicated non-verbally. Your body language, dress sense and appearance shout: "This person is a champion" or "a flop."

Effective communication often starts with a person realising its importance in helping to reach or not reach goals, be it making those essential business contacts or clinching lucrative contracts.

Communication can be likened to a skeleton key which can unlock doors of opportunity during a variety of different circumstances. For example, a person's punctuality can transmit silent but powerful messages. When meeting a potential business partner who can earn you a healthy sum, strolling up half an hour late for an appointment will communicate a disrespectful and even a rude attitude. Punctuality, on the other hand, conveys the opposite.

A shrewd business person will recognize the value of not only communicating but planning a communication strategy. When meeting a potential client for the first time, he will carry out the necessary research into the individual's personality, his history, future goals and the company profile. Knowledge is power, and gaining insight into a potential client will enable an entrepreneur to be aware of how he can best come to some kind of business arrangement.

Preparing a communication strategy is all about trying to take the time to understand the person you hope to do business with. When this is achieved, business colleagues can be communicated with on a level which will enable you to be viewed as a potential friend.

Now, you may be thinking, "I don't want friends, I want to boost profits!" The relevance of being on friendly terms with potential business partners is that decision-makers tend to buy people, not the products. If you are liked because of your effective communication skills and display a personal interest towards your client, the chances of success will grow a hundredfold.

When you are meeting a person for the first time, asking yourself a few questions will contribute to success. For example: what sort of meeting will you be attending, formal or informal, and how will the other person or persons be dressed? In general, most people are comfortable when they are around people like themselves.

And so, if you have an appointment with the bank manager to finance a property deal, leave the cap and T-shirt at home if you don't want to be viewed as a joker. Dress smart!

Remember, outside the music and fashion businesses, it is inappropriate to dress like a fashion victim. Save the Versace and Cavalli wear for the evening and weekend raves.

In conclusion: dress for where we you are going, not where you are.

What about your body language? If you are a habitual slouch, what image will this convey? I can imagine your prospective business partners will be thinking: "Is this guy for real? If he doesn't have enough energy to keep his body erect, how on earth can he help my business to grow?"

By making it a habit to sit up, the impression you will convey to your future business associates will be: "This guy is on the ball."

And since we are discussing the topic of balls, eye contact is also very important. It has often been said that the windows to a person's heart and mind are his eyes. By maintaining respectful eye contact, you can convey conviction in your business venture, skills and or service.

One word of caution! Do not stare. If you are male and stare at a woman too intensely, you may be viewed as a weirdo, with the potential to become a stalker. And if you stare at the wrong person in the wrong part of town, it could result in an aggressive so-and-so snarling: "Who you looking at? Do you want some?" (ie, a couple of swollen eyes or even worse!)

# Chapter 26

## WHO SAYS CRIME DON'T PAY?

Arguing the pros and cons (excuse the pun!) of 'Who Says Crime Don't Pay' is a controversial business.

The majority of criminals who find themselves locked up for a stretch or who have received heavy fines for various petty misdemeanours will dispute the title of this Chapter. The average law-abiding citizen will also refute that any real benefits can be enjoyed through criminal methods.

But in reality there is always a minority who slip through the legal net and will beg to differ. This minority may include drug dealers, fraudsters, extortionists or the old fashioned armed robber, welding a shot gun. Yes they are still around! In December 2004, for example, £26.5m was stolen from the Northern Bank in Northern Ireland during one of the biggest cash robbery's in UK history. The majority of the robbers haven't been charged, neither has the cash been recovered and is probably being used to fund drugs smuggling and terrorism.

But this chapter is emphasising that criminal activity doesn't always involve 'cons' in a traditional sense. We all know that some of the biggest blags in history have involved governments invading lands to rape, pillage and kill under the pretence of some form of legality.

The record of big business isn't much cleaner than that of many governments. Have you ever tried to make an insurance claim, for example? You may have religiously put money aside to insure goods for years and yet when a claim is made the best solicitors will be employed to ensure you don't receive a dime, and to make matters worse, you will be given a thousand and one different excuses as to why you are not going to get your money back.

Under normal circumstances, if a person pays for a service that is not delivered, the act comes under the category of daylight robbery. But a minority can get away with 'legal theft'. This minority will then turn around and preach: "Do as I say and not as I do."

The problem with the average person in business is that they fail to do as 'they do' and follow the example of the elite, who employ the most skilful accountants, lawyers, barristers and other specialist advisors to find loopholes in the law to hold on to their power and money.

Instead of interpreting the law and allowing brilliant lawyers and accountants to protect and boost finances, far too many businessmen see legislation in black and white, rather than those grey areas that can be used to their advantage.

By failing to interpret the law, a businessman is allowing himself to remain in a financial rut, rather than moving upwards by thinking and existing outside the box. While paying for top-class advisors can be an expensive business, in the long run they reap dividends for the upwardly mobile entrepreneur.

Empowerment isn't advocating that the law should be broken, because without the legal establishment there would be anarchy, which would choke good business. But it is questioning what constitutes a crime in our society, given how some of the most powerful institutions get away with day-light robbery.

# Chapter 27

## LONG-TERM STRATEGY

For Empowerment's intellectual readers, few experiences will beat uttering the word 'checkmate' and observing the look of disbelief on your opponent's face before he crumples in a heap.

I'm not saying that the readers of this book have a leaning towards sadism, although there may be a few! More apt is the satisfaction of being able to observe how your brilliant operation unravels, you steal the show from your opponent before his eyes and you finally pat yourself on the back and exclaim: "Bloody genius!"

Having a long-term strategy in business will enable you to enjoy a similar euphoria. By being a number of moves ahead of your competitors, associates and or enemies you will always be able to win the game and silently whisper those words: "Checkmate, mate."

Before you can be one step ahead in the game or able to strategise, you have to know who you are dealing with and get into the mind of your opponent. This doesn't mean taking a degree in psychology, but it does mean asking yourself some basic questions, and they are basic.

Every action causes a reaction. Fact. And so you need to ask yourself: what are the likely reactions of your opponent, in given situations? What are his tendencies? Was he bred for fighting--excuse the expression--and does he, like an American Pit Bull Terrier, just love to get his teeth into something at the drop of a hat?

Or maybe your opponent is like the paranoid cokehead. His problem is that he doesn't have to sniff the white stuff for his suspicions to unhinge his fragile mental state. Generally he flips as quickly as flipping a pancake, although he may not always show it externally.

Then there is the small stump character that has an Idi Amin syndrome. The more you try to wrestle a bit of power from his hands, the more he will hold on to the figurative reins of power. Usually there are two ways of dealing with the 'dictator' type: hitting him over the head with a heavy blunt instrument; or fooling him into believing that he is in control while he panders to your scheme. But beware: if the bluff is uncovered you will either need to go into hiding or invest in some body armour!

The point is that once you know the personality profile of your opponent, you can predict with a measure of accuracy how he will respond when you send out your bait.

As a general rule, people follow similar patterns of behaviour, unless they are complete lunatics. Once you can ascertain what type of personality an opponent has, then you can strategise what his next move is going to be in a given situation. An ability to predict what your opponent's next move is will enable you to counteract this before it happens. In other words, you will be in the driving seat and will be able to carry out your business objective.

A useful tip: while your business objective should be clear in mind, prepare a strategy that is flexible and which will enable you to reach a reasonable agreement. As you map out your long-term strategy, never forget the battle is won or lost in the mind.

## Chapter 28

## PROPAGANDA AND BIAS

We have all heard the expression 'the pen is mightier than the sword', meaning that words and communication, when properly used, can be more effective in convincing the awkward soul than violence. But I wonder how many entrepreneurs really appreciate how deep the above idiom is?

For example, what makes more sense: getting a clueless so-and-so to do what you want by hypnotising with lyrics, or beating him into submission, with the prospect of having a return match with a snarling armed beast? The answer is obvious.

For the above reason, the powerful have used and will always use propaganda to keep the masses in shape, from the likes of Hitler to the likes of Tony Blair. Sorry to have to include the ex-Prime Minister in the same sentence with the ex-fascist, but there you go!

When Tony Blair's ten-year tenure in office is analysed, commentators frequently comment on his party's ability to spin or to manipulate public opinion in favour of Labour's cause. What of the former Prime Minister's sidekick during his glory days: Alistair Campbell, the Labour Party's ex-director of communications or spin doctor. He was often described as the real Deputy Prime Minister and the second most powerful man in the UK at the time.

In our modern times, politicians, celebrities and business people always court those in the media to get their way, through progaganda! For example, the British political party that wins the heart of Rupert Murdoch, the owner of newspapers such as the Sun and the Times, has access to millions of minds and loyal supporters. At the other extreme, Richard Branson is always conjuring up some pioneering scheme which will be jumped on by media darlings, with the result the profile of the Virgin brand is heightened. It's called good public relations.

On a more sinister note, the powers that be may use fear tactics to coerce you into doing what they want. How often have you been confronted by one of those letters or reminders: "Pay your TV License or else! Or else a whopping great fine."

This illustrates why those at the helm of business should scrutinise the media and other sources of information they are exposed to and can manipulate. By being aware of the political stance of newspapers, for example, the information a businessman reads and uses can be validated or at least interpreted. The same is true of any information being sourced and used.

Successful business people need to acquire the knack of generating good propaganda and bias, to beat off enemies when necessary. Doing so can be the difference between being a victim of propaganda and manipulation or not, and being a follower or a leader.

Charles Gordon: "A leader will see what is going on around him and will use it to his benefit, while a follower will just do what is going on."

# Chapter 29

## HAVE A BROAD UNDERSTANDING OF EVERY AREA

Despite the common notion of the jack-of-all-trades being a waste of space, the acquisition of a broad understanding of different areas of business has a valuable place in the arsenal of the man or woman who is empowered.

The person who bothers to acquire a broad understanding in business is like the individual who possesses all the different bits of a jigsaw puzzle, pieces them together and is then able to appreciate the bigger picture. The businessman who grasps the bigger picture will always be able to successfully assemble and direct projects under his oversight.

But being a jack-of-all-trades also prevents an entrepreneur from being held at the mercy of advisors who may not always have the best interests of their wealthy and all too trusting clients at heart.

Earlier in this book the chapter 'Let Passion Drive You' highlighted the importance of self-motivation if entrepreneurs are to make their dreams a reality. But along with passion, a measure of theory, such as interpreting the law, is essential to prevent an entrepreneur driving along the wrong side of the road and falling foul of the law. For example, in 2005 one of the richest Black men in Europe at the time, Carl Cushnie, received a six-year sentence for fraud. His company, Versailles, inflated its turnover in order to receive huge loans and to hike the value of the company on the stock market. The bottom line is that Carl Cushnie was found guilty of pocketing millions of pounds illegally, and received a prison sentence as a result.

Carl Cushnie, the first Black businessman to appear in the Sunday Times Rich List, said he knew nothing about the fraud and it was down to his finance director, Frederick Clough. Also unknown to Cushnie was that his 'buddy' stole £19m from his company.

Cushnie's experience, if true, underscores the importance of having a broad understanding of every area of business, particularly your own, to avoid the snare of being overly reliant on advisors.

While it is doubtful that many of the readers of this book will end up in prison because of failing to become a jack-of-all-trades, nonetheless it can result in the loss of profits. Few advisors will passionately defend an entrepreneur's realm if they sense that he is not on the ball mentally. To bridge the gap between ignorance and a basic knowledge of different facets of business, simply attend a short course, topped up with a selection of suitable books and lunches with those who are in the know.

# Chapter 30

## THE KEY IS NOT WHEN TO BUY, BUT WHEN TO SELL

To avoid a venture eventually becoming a drain on your hard-earned resources, never forget one of the keys to financial empowerment is not so much when to buy, but when to sell.

Before making any kind of investment, drum this into your head and set it in stone: "As soon as the goose gets fat and plump--or, in other words, reaches its peak--I'm going to sell it for as much as I can."

Good timing in most activities in life is important, but in business it is essential.

While the timing of when to buy a company, service or asset is frequently discussed, of far greater value is selling these at just the right moment. Knowing when to sell is the difference between success and failure, profit and loss.

The problem with a lot of would-be money-makers is that far too often they forget what time it is, because of being side-tracked!

Entrepreneurs, like anyone else, can allow their hearts to rule their heads, causing them to minimise the bottom-line, which is to make a profit from a particular venture.

The art of knowing when to sell is identifying when the business is at its peak. Possessing a sound understanding of your market is invaluable if you are to time a sale well. For example, if an investor in the property market holds on to his portfolio until a recession kicks in, he may find that his investment, which was worth its weight in gold, is now worth peanuts. Deciding before money is ploughed into a project the amount you are happy to earn helps in making a final decision as to when to sell.

A lot of entrepreneurs make the mistake of holding on to an investment for a little longer than they should, until it turns the figurative corner and becomes a liability. In effect they become little more than glorified gamblers, who after winning a small stake refuse to quit until they leave the casino with empty pockets, flat broke.

Experienced entrepreneurs believe that most ventures have a three-to-five-year life span--mild growth in the first two years, followed by a period when the business should explode, between the third and fifth year. It is during this period of rapid growth that the entrepreneur should be finding another parent for his business.

While the sale of a company can cause its founder to experience the shakes, successful entrepreneurs are business pioneers who recognise that all developing companies get to the point when they need bigger structures, more funding and organisations to back them. Unless a business brings new minds into a project, that refresh and motivate, then it's inevitably going to reach a natural end.

Of course, not to be forgotten are the joys of passing on a healthy, vibrant company at its peak. A shrewd negotiator can carve out a sale that will result in a win-win situation--call it a golden handshake.

When selling a founding company some of the options to consider, ensuring that revenue continues to flow is to sell the controlling percentage of the company or to be employed as a consultant. The above suggestions provide income without the financial risk if anything goes wrong.

The above package is what Clive Calder negotiated when selling Zomba Music for £2.74 billion, to BMG in 2002, netting £1.23 billion in the process. An interesting twist to the sale was that Zomba had exercised what was described as a "put" option with BMG, effectively requiring the German major to buy the remaining shares it did not own in Clive Calder's group; at its peak price during the mid 1990's.

Clive Calder the South African billionaire is aware that to remain empowered the 'key is not knowing when to buy, but when to sell."

# Chapter 31

## CONCEAL YOUR INTENTIONS

Those who fail to conceal their intentions as they attempt to climb the ladder of success will inevitably have the ladder swept away from beneath them.

While ambition is generally viewed as a positive quality, for those in power it can cause alarm signals, and who can blame them! History books are filled with examples of the ambitious who have left a trail of blood in their rise to the top. The ambitious can be extremely dangerous!

It is hardly surprising, then, that the powerful are constantly looking warily over their shoulders to defend themselves against the latest upstart (real or imagined), who may be eager to snatch their throne.

In business folklore it is alleged that Mohamed al-Fayed concealed his attentions like a true professional in his relationship as the Sultan of Brunei's financial advisor, during the mid 1980's. After an enquiry following al-Fayed's takeover of the House of Fraser in 1985, for £615m, the Department of Trade said: "We are satisfied that the image created between November 1984 and March 1985 of their (al-Fayed's) wealthy Egyptian ancestors was completely bogus. The evidence pointing to Brunei is very strong indeed."

Although the Sultan of Brunei gave the Harrods owner power of attorney to buy the Dorchester Hotel on his behalf, he said he didn't give him permission to use his finance to put a deposit on his purchase of the House of Frazer. The Egyptian businessman has always claimed that he bought the retail establishment with his families cash!

If an individual is going to rise to the top he must learn to exercise self-control, dampening the fears of those in power rather than adding fuel to the fire.

When an upstart makes it apparent that he or she wants to be like the person at the top, their attempt at flattery may backfire or, at the minimum, be a waste of time. Generally, people who have obtained power want to keep it and will seldom reveal the secrets behind their success, unless they are 70 and have no alternative but to pass the baton over to someone else.

At this point I would like to inject a measure of caution. While we all have talents and display a measure of ambition, if a person vocalises this too much and is arrogant about their abilities, they had better look out! The person who you thought would help you will also take pleasure in sweeping the figurative ladder away from the ground so that you collapse in a heap.

To prevent a premature fall from grace, it is important that in your demeanour you show you are not the type that believes money maketh the man. In other words avoid a gravalicious (hungry, greedy) attitude.

As you start to climb the ladder of success and power, don't bite off the hand that extends opportunities to you in eagerness. As six-figure sums are bandied around, don't jump around and react like an excited kid, but keep a dignified attitude.

Concealing your intentions can also be achieved by occasionally diverting attention from hard talk and showing a genuine interest in those at the top. Try to become their friends, since they will probably have few real buddies. Talk about hobbies and interests that you both enjoy, similarities in culture and family background--anything that will prevent the man from assuming that you are just a gold-digger after the crown!

Once the person in power no longer regards you as a threat, wait for the business opportunities to roll your way, and if you have a venture or two that you require assistance with, always highlight the benefits that will be enjoyed by them. After all, you have his best interest at heart!

Never forget all the diplomacy that was invested in acquiring your powerful allies. This will prevent you from losing useful contacts that can help you, because of becoming overly familiar in business practices or in your general demeanour.

Concealing intentions also has its place when one is dealing with financial institutions such as banks. At times, if a particular bank manager views you as too successful, you may not receive the support you expect, particularly if he is on a measly salary. It is shrewd at times to conceal the immediate trappings of your success--Rolex watch etc--to make the poor man feel a bit better about himself. Remember, once you have acquired a measure of wealth, not everyone has your best interests at heart.

## Chapter 32

## KNOW YOUR WORTH

The man who fails to place a healthy and realistic value on himself will soon discover that others will do the same.

While knowing your worth can do wonders for the ego, it can have the same effect on one's bank balance, contributing to a person's empowerment.

Alan Sugar, the businessman, was rebuffed on a number of occasions as he sold tape recorders to his employers as junior. He is quoted as saying: "Rather than slogging my heart out to sell someone a single machine, it dawned on me that I could earn much more for the same (or possibly less) effort if I targeted the chief buyer at Curry's and aimed for larger orders of, say, 1000 units."

Despite his attempts at enterprise The Apprentice star was penalized for the special discounts his boss gave to larger customers – even though he was making a healthy profit as a result of his deal with Sugar.

Looking back at his decision to walk out on his former employers the entrepreneur said:"Those bosses did me a favour. Had they not been so ungrateful, I might still be working for one of them today. Instead, they made me determined to work for myself."

Calculating one's financial worth can also enable an entrepreneur to avoid mundane activities that can deprive them of valuable time and, of course, income. For example, would it make financial sense for Bill Gates, the Microsoft chairman, who earns thousands of pounds an hour, to use too much of his precious time on routine matters when he could use those valuable hours to help develop the next Window's operating system or other gizmo?

For a person to know their hourly worth isn't as difficult as it may appear. With calculator in hand, simply add up your monthly income and then divide this by the number of days in the month, and then by 24. Do not be startled if your hourly worth is the minimum wage, of £5.05 an hour, at the local McDonald's fast food restaurant. There is hope!

An individual's awareness of their monetary worth, particularly if it's Just Over Broke, can be a motivator to plan ahead, with the goal of entering a vocation or a business that will eventually increase earning potential.

A word of caution for any aspiring Bill Gates's: don't price yourself out of the market by entertaining too many delusions of grandeur. At times it may be beneficial to play smart, by pricing yourself below competitors to generate more work and income in the process.

# Chapter 33

## PLAY DUMBER THAN YOUR MARK

The Spanish Baroque writer Baltasar Gracian is quoted as saying: "Superiority of a subject over his prince is not only stupid, it is fatal. This is a lesson that the stars in the sky teach us -they may be related to the sun and just as brilliant, but they never appear in her company."

Empowerment has turned the table on business strategy with the chapter 'Play Dumber Than Your Mark'.

While the majority of business schools would happily promote the concept 'Tell the world that you're the best', a more cautious approach will result in longevity. Experience suggests that bosses can be very insecure and will often insist on being the top dog.

One of the most vital lessons contained in 'Play Dumber Than Your Mark' is that to outshine the shining star can prove a fatal mistake. While a person may experience a measure of gratitude by blowing his own trumpet, in the long run it can end up with a person being used as target practice by his superior. Isn't it logical that there can only be one man or woman at the top?

A discerning king will be aware that ambitious upstarts will be drooling when imagining wearing his crown and all the trappings that go along with this. Survival dictates, therefore, that you take this into consideration and even tone down your natural abilities which, if not subdued, can cause the poisoned arrows to be heading in your direction.

Diplomacy and patience are tactics that are necessary if anyone is to rise to the top of their field. They allow the man who wears the crown to become sufficiently comfortable around an apprentice, to no longer view him as a threat, and to willingly share some of his glory. On the other hand, if he or she is a paranoid megalomaniac, the Trojan Horse technique can be used to secretly gather contacts, contracts and much more. This technique can eventually result in an individual creating their own empire, outside of their ever-watchful senior.

The coup is the final option. But beware, there are rarely bloodless coups, and if you fail you may end up not only cash-strapped, but also with a reputation that stinks! In other words you may be permanently labelled a disloyal, greedy git who is willing to stab anyone in the back, even the person who puts food on your table.

To 'Play Dumber Than Your Mark' is an art that few master. Yes, those in power who you are trying to impress need to be aware that you are not a simpleton, but neither should they be disturbed by the fact that you possess knowledge that surpasses their own. To avoid this it is often beneficial to display a little knowledge about a lot of different topics, so you do not blatantly outshine the master.

The 1970's TV detective character Colombo used deception masterfully. His image was that of an inoffensive, confused type, an act that always fooled the prime suspect into a false sense of security. Eventually, with his defences somewhat down, it caused him to carelessly reveal vital pieces of evidence which would always lead to his downfall.

The above reveals that it is usually more beneficial to say less than to play the big man. Not only does it prevent causing offence too frequently and the uncovering of your own weak spots, but it enables the gathering of vital intelligence on the sector that you eventually want to dominate.

# Chapter 34

## CHOOSE YOUR BATTLES

In the field of war, those who fail to choose their battles wisely end up in a box.

In the field of business, an 'all-guns-blazing' approach may not always cause a person's family to book an early appointment with a funeral director, but it will cause a person to end up trapped in society's symbolic box.

When a person learns to choose his battles in the business arena, the web of financial snares that society reels out can be avoided by acquiring the ability to stand back rationally, even coldly, to assess the financial viability of a project.

The successful avoid the knee-jerk reaction of the 'green', who often jump feet first into every project that is put on a plate, without asking the vital question: "Will it boost my power?"

Learning to prevent your heart ruling your head is easier said than done, but will always mean the difference between you getting stuck in trench warfare or making forward momentum in the battles you choose. To think rationally, always know your goal and how you will reach it. Ask yourself: will this project be a good use of time or a waste of time? Is it the right time for an all-out attack or is the market not ready for my service or product?

Once you are convinced a project is worth pursuing, identify a rich and reliable power source and then plug into it--the movers and shakers, who hold the purse strings--to get the deal off the ground. To oil this process an entrepreneur should strive to meet people outside his financial and class bracket, who can empower them. The message is network, network, and network!

Simply put, becoming empowered is all about focusing on the big kill.

As you network, identify sources that in the long run will be able to recharge or replenish your reputation, your financial status, your power.

The powerful have always treasured the art of skilfully biding their time, either to earn a profit or to remove their enemies who are a pain.

Choosing your battles is not always easy when the world is filled with competitors, who experience great pleasure in attempting to knock you off your pretty perch or screwing you for as much as they can get away with. For the inexperienced man in power, the result can be fighting battles 24/7, rather than choosing them.

To avoid becoming a victim, you must imitate the attitude of the wealthy. Have you noticed how the powerful always put defence mechanisms in place to reduce the number of battles they are forced to engage in? Frequently, the wealthy ensure that their enemies cannot get to them in the first place. You can speak to his personal assistant, his press officer or lawyer, but you can't speak to the main man when you have a matter to settle and it drives you mad!

Defence mechanisms do not have to be set up at great cost. For example, starting limited trading companies offer limited liability and will disarm those who are intent on grabbing some of your personal assets.

To set up protective barriers, invest in a good accountant and lawyer. They can save you vital time, energy, money and stress.

Charles Gordon: "You need to get the right balance when fighting battles, otherwise you will be chasing your tail with nothing to show for it."

# Chapter 35

## ORGANISATION AND ORDER

Charles Gordon: "Successful businesses are based on organisation and order, without which they will be mayhem. People don't fail, systems fail."

An examination of any powerful institution, from the Sony Records to Shell plc, will uncover the importance of a clearly defined hierarchy and business plan.

The concept of organisation and order may sound extremely dull to many, but without strong systems in place, be it work ethics or job criteria, business empires cannot be built and maintained.

In simple terms: without organisation and order, your power will simply trickle out of your palms as you are trampled on and mayhem will become king.

Can you imagine, for example, if there were no laws in society? The ruling class would lose their authority and it would simply be chaos! People would drive on the wrong side of the road, taxes would not be paid, and crime would be rampant! (Does this description appear uncomfortably close to society today?)

To preserve your authority or status as a man of influence, it is wise to remember that many of your employees or associates may be power crazy or damn lazy. Clearly defined hierarchy and job criteria will help you to monitor the abilities and motives of those around you, as well as providing motivating direction.

As you become Empowered and climb the ladder of success,

you will notice that the need for organisation and order will increase. Yet when you honestly look at yourself you may have to admit something - that you are an unorganised, messy so and so and need to change your habits.

If the above description is the cap that fits, there is reason to worry, since no business can succeed without a decent structure. Nonetheless there is no reason to give up. There is hope! After making an assessment of yourself -- your strengths and weaknesses -- consider whom you can draft in to fill the gaps and to transform your image from one of disarray to one of a sleek organisation.

It has been observed that the stronger a team within an organisation and the better their ability to follow through on orders, the more stable will be its power base. A strong power-base has numerous benefits to an individual who is acquiring power. Just like a literal foundation helps to absorb the pressures thrust upon a building, good organisation can enable a company to thrive, even during shaky financial or internal periods.

But a strong power base or organisation pattern also provides a springboard for a rapid expansion. Why do you think some of the most successful companies such as Tesco, McDonalds and Starbucks are taking over the high street? It is because they recognise the importance of good systems and replicate these mercilessly, sweeping past everything in their path.

Organisation has another benefit. It affords the luxury of greater efficiency and something most of us yearn for, less work! It has been recognised that by investing a small amount of time each day on planning your activities, your workload can be reduced considerably, and of course another bonus will be less stress.

There are some pitfalls to watch out for when implementing organisation and order. When a company or person becomes too orderly and systematic, the personal touch and attention to detail can quickly be lost. Do not forget that a service that displays a measure of personal appeal and attention will be far more appreciated than one that is predictable and/or robotic.

# Chapter 36

## NO MAN IS AN ISLAND

If there was an opportunity to own a continent or island, what would you choose? Some might answer: "Give me an island any day. They are beautiful, usually possess tropical climates, and of course I wouldn't have to deal with those urban ferrets that make my life a misery." But the downside could be the exposure to mind numbing levels of boredom. If you have ever visited a 'paradise' island you will be aware of how quickly you can drive around them and after a week or so experience rigor mortis (get bored stiff).

There would be no such a problem if you owned a continent, because of the varieties on offer--foods, climates, music--it would simply be great.

Of course the references to owning continents and islands are all far-fetched, even for the readers of Empowerment, but the concepts can be applied to business.

Once you have started trading, what will you opt for: a Robinson Crusoe-type business existence, veering on isolation, or something that is a bit more expansive?

Some entrepreneurs will answer this question by shouting: "I want my business to be a treasure-island."

Of course, the island mentality is based on the premise that success in business hinges on the owner maintaining a high level of control and ownership, and he may think that anything else results in a lacklustre work ethic, coupled with rubbish performance and results.

The Robinson Crusoe character may also prefer the hands-on approach, which is commendable, but the problem is that he will eventually be smacked in the face by a big problem. He will only be in the position to run a small business, because no matter how great an entrepreneur he is, tackling all the tasks of running a thriving company on his own will simply be too much. In business, the statement 'no man is an island' is for real.

One of the secrets of empowerment is knowing which reins of power to release, when, and to what extent. Can you imagine riding a powerful stallion, for example, and holding on to its reins so tightly that the horse's ability to let rip was constantly stifled? The horse would eventually freak out because of frustration and decide to give you a couple of stamps with his hooves for good measure. At the other extreme, if this powerful beast were in full flight, would it be wise to let go of its reins altogether or allow free rein? If you did, the end result would be a rapid flight in mid-air which would end with you landing on your head!

To avoid various frustrations and dangers in business, a long-term strategy of growth, which will eventually provide the freedom and flexibility to delve into other projects, is the ideal. Of course, to enjoy this luxury you need to delegate, by willingly training individuals who will eventually take over the reins of power.

The success of the Virgin Group is down to the strategy of No Man is an Island, allowing the company to establish a variety of subgroups – Virgin Atlantic Airways, Virgin Records, Virgin Express, Virgin Cola, Virgin Vodka and many others.

Of course you must be careful who you choose as an apprentice, when applying the model of No Man is an Island. If you select the wrong person your business will soon be their business, or they may be your best competitor with inside knowledge of your operation...

And remember, delegating is not a swear word. Okay, your apprentice may not be as knowledgeable, efficient, articulate, brilliant and handsome as you, but they are giving you the necessary time to spy out other ventures that will allow the business to become a continent, rather than remaining an island.

# Chapter 37

## TAILOR THE JOB TO EACH PERSON'S STRENGTHS

For a company boss, trying to slot the correct person into the correct job may at times appear like trying to force a square peg into a round hole--a tiresome and problematic effort.

Persevering so that the correct candidate is eventually found to fill a vital role in a company is well worth the effort and can be the difference between having a figurative spanner in the works to someone who proves to be a vital cog in your business machinery.

The question which thousands of business people increasingly ask is: "How do I find that vital cog which will contribute to the smooth running of my business?"

The traditional view is to create a job description once a position is available and the victim has to adhere to this whether they like it or not. The downside to this is that employees don't like their jobs, hate their bosses and at the end of the week shout: "Thank God it's Friday."

The problem with forcing square staff into a round hole is that they are neither creative nor productive in their roles and the company's morale ends up about as flat as a pancake.

Some hard-nosed slave drivers may think: "Who cares! We can't all do jobs that leave us on cloud nine. Isn't it obvious that some poor soul has to sweat in the sweatshop, as long as it's not me, of course!" But modern-day slavery is a short-sighted way of running a business, and eventually results in the wheels of a company grinding sluggishly along rather than running smoothly because they are well oiled by a satisfied and happy staff.

To avoid an unhappy, unlucky and unproductive workforce, it's important that those in power strive to tailor jobs to each person's strengths. Some people may argue: "Isn't that what drafting a job description and the interview process is all about?" The reality of the working environment is that just because a person can do the job competently, it doesn't mean that he or she isn't a latent genius in other areas, which can eventually help to boost a company's profits.

The creative boss will try to suss out not only what makes his staff tick, but also how he can develop their potential. Unfortunately there are no short cuts to understanding the strengths and weaknesses of members of your master team.

Some companies simply throw their new employees into the deep end of various departments, such as accounts, sales or public relations, to discover if they sink or swim. After three months of testing the waters it should be clear how a company's operation can tailor a job to the new bright spark's strengths.

Generally speaking a couture product is more comfortable, efficient and durable than a ready-to-wear item. Similar benefits can be enjoyed when creative companies tailor jobs to employees' strengths.

# Chapter 38

## WHAT IS A NETWORK?

Charles Gordon: "A business person without a network isn't a business person."

There is a popular saying that to get ahead in life what's most important is not what you know, but who you know.

Sad to say, far too many people waste valuable time hitting their heads against figurative glass ceilings, getting all battered and bruised, when they could simply use the key of networking to go through the door of opportunity.

The reality of life is that although a brilliant business mind may theoretically know how to earn a million selling a particular product or service, trying to pry open the doors that will make it all happen is a completely different challenge. An effective network can bridge the gap.

The rich and powerful use their networks all the time to transform theory into reality. For example, Mark Thatcher the son of an ex-British Prime Minister, Margaret Thatcher, was alleged to have used family contacts to earn £12m as a broker in the Al-Yamamah arms deal with the Saudi-Arabian Government, in 1985. Mark Thatcher denies receiving payment. George Bush used family contacts to become the American President in 2001.

In essence, your network or contacts are the keys that are used when necessary to unlock those doors of opportunity. These individuals of influence are persons who can say to the doorkeeper: "If you scratch my back, you know I'll scratch yours, and what's more, I can vouch for this guy's credibility."

But contacts are not only needed when trying to enter the door of opportunity. As a business grows, it becomes less likely that the top man will personally have all the necessary connections to ensure the smooth functioning of his operation. If his inner circle of advisors has any real clout they should be able to draw on 'known' talents from outside to ensure the task at hand is carried out.

Scouring the Yellow Pages or placing an ad in a local job centre is generally a no-no, particularly when trying to tie up deals that are time-sensitive. The same holds true when an important or sensitive project is about to be cracked. It's generally more advantageous to invite a 'known' person through your door of opportunity to ensure the task is not only carried out, but carried out well.

Ultimately a person of influence or power should be able to make one or two phone calls from his network to get the wheels of his next venture in motion.

To acquire a network it's obvious that networking has to be carried out. View it as a long-term investment which can help to earn healthy profits by clinching deals and developing formidable reputations.

# Chapter 39

## HOW TO LEAD A TEAM

Any team is only as good as its leader. But how do you lead a team which may traditionally view those at the top as 'them', rather than 'one of us'.

The challenge is a serious one because all too often strained relations between managers and staff results in an unhappy and unproductive work environment, which can damage profits in the process.

How many companies have become infested with moaning, groaning and a lazy spirit on the job? The led often reason: "If my boss doesn't care a hoot about my needs and is leading me like a lamb to the slaughter, I'm going to treat him exactly the same to see how he likes it."

The astute power broker breaks the tit-for-tat cycle by winning the support and loyalty of his team, rather than antagonising them by using the heavy-handed, distant approach. His logic is: "Why breed enemies when I can court supporters who will see what a wonderful guy I am and reinforce, even protect my power at the top?"

To be a successful team leader, an entrepreneur must become a skilled puppeteer who knows what strings to pull within his organisation to produce the desired results on the business stage. In other words, the team leader must discern if and how each team player will react as he pulls their string. Will they respond vigorously to his direction, with lethargy, or stubbornly resist?

To answer these questions, the man at the top has to get to know the dynamics within his team. In every group there are leaders and followers. A team leader needs to discover the strengths and weaknesses of his group, who has the potential to be his right-hand man, and how they interact with each other. Is the team like a well-honed human body that works harmoniously, or is it a bit cancerous because of in-fighting, and if so what is causing this?

Given that a bit of friction between staff members is inevitable, an astute leader will adopt a company mission statement to encourage each team player to pull together in the same direction because of having a common goal. Mind you not all friction is bad, particularly if it creates a measure of friendly competition that pushes the team an extra mile.

For the man who rushes from one business meeting to the next, getting to know his team well is easier said than done. But just as a busy executive will invest some of his precious time in assessing his market and the state of the economy to keep one step ahead of his competition, he has to do exactly the same in getting to know his team well and what motivates them. It's well worth the effort! Half an hour spent regularly speaking to members of the team to consider their needs and express your appreciation and concern for their efforts should be viewed as an investment, not a waste of time, which can reap long-term results in greater productivity and more income.

The message that needs to be conveyed is that people at the top need to care for the people on the rungs below, and as long as they care, their managers and supervisors will care, which ultimately lead to better productivity. People need to feel as though they are part of a team, not a dictatorship, where there is a power struggle.

Once a team leader becomes familiar with the qualities of his team he can then build company logistics around the strengths and preferences of those under his wings, rather than doing the reverse. When team players perform in positions they are most happy and comfortable in, they will readily respond when their figurative strings are pulled by their boss, rather than drag their feet in protest.

The boss who adopts the "haute couture" recruitment policy when putting together his team is opting for a premier work ethic. Not only will staff members work harder, but also customer service will excel because the most talented team players are being used on any given assignment. The "haute couture" work ethic will not only cause soaring profits, but boost company morale, because the team avoids being slowly poisoned by a toxic environment caused by moaning, bitching, angry and ultimately unhappy colleagues.

Despite trying to adopt a caring attitude within your team, this has to be balanced with a disciplined approach. Some people will self-correct and can analyse and see where the problems are, while for others a firmer hand will be needed.

A skilled leader will not over-exert authority pissing people off in the process, but will be fair and firm. Your actions should have an awareness that your team is only as strong as its weakest link, and that one person can bring the team down and discredit the whole company.

A word of caution for team leaders: don't be lazy and just assume that big bucks will make your team members happy, because this isn't always the case. Even when a person prostitutes themselves for higher amounts of money they may not always be happy in the long-run if they are in an unwanted role. Within six months they may not be able to hide their unhappiness behind their new Gucci range and can begin to drag their feet when receiving a gentle tug from the boss.

# Chapter 40

## REWARD GOOD BEHAVIOUR

"If a flower is watered, it flourishes. If not, it shrivels up and dies." (Richard Branson – The Importance of Being Richard Branson')

By rewarding a team's efforts, a boss allows his team to reward him with a work ethos that will become the bedrock of a successful trading company. It doesn't take rocket science to work out that staff who are appreciated by the powers that be will be more loyal, happy, and industrious than those who are ill-treated.

For company heads that frowned after reading 'Reward Good Behaviour', relax! A reward doesn't always have to be the six-figure bonuses which are dished out by the likes of Goldman Sachs and JP Morgan. But if your golden boy or girl is earning you a tidy sum, why not keep them happy by recognising their brilliance, while ensuring your profit margins will continue to be bullish? The message is: be reasonable. You're not the only one who should enjoy la dolce vita (the sweet life).

Sad to say, not enough bosses show by their actions that basic truth that everyone needs to feel valued, and scratch their heads in bemusement when a steady stream of staff leave for competing companies or don't give two hoots about the business. In most western countries even the most uninformed employee is aware that slavery has been abolished!

It's generally recognised that corporate UK has a culture which isn't too keen on dishing out bonuses, and has the attitude: "I've given you a job, haven't I? What more do you want?" But any boss of a privately-owned company who has any measure of long-term vision will recognise that it is in his best interest to reward his team, especially the whizz kid.

But appreciating brilliance and hard work doesn't always mean transferring large sums of money into bank accounts. The shrewd tactician will be aware that reward systems should be applied with great subtlety and skill. After all, why give a large bonus to your bespectacled academic genius, when he is not motivated by finance and would prefer investment to research a particular project, for example?

The key to using the rewards ethos to boost the overall performance of the business is knowing what makes your team tick. By being observant and a good communicator, a company head will be aware which team players get a kick from financial reward, and which from an expression of verbal appreciation or increased responsibility, in order to hit the right button of motivation.

But for the man at the top to get the best from his team, he has to be more than a master of discernment and has to have that genuine desire for his team to reach their full potential, both financially and otherwise. Such a display of personal interest will ensure a work ethic among staff that they will always go the extra mile, which will be the difference between success and failure in business.

# Chapter 41

## OBJECTION HANDLING

How a customer's objections are handled will ensure whether a person either stays on board or shouts: "Mutiny! Jump ship!" From a customer's point of view, how an objection is handled often calls for such drastic action or not.

In an ideal world, objection handling is an essential part of customer satisfaction, and should whisper consolingly to the customer: 'I appreciate your financial loyalty and will try my best to solve your problem. Stay on board.'

In the real world, objections are frequently dealt with by the heart rather than the mind, resulting in an emotional mess.

Confronted by an angry and dissatisfied client, an entrepreneur may not verbally respond by saying: "How dare you speak to me like that?" or "If you don't like it you know what you can do, don't you?" The problem could be in the manner in which an issue is dealt with. If an objection is not dealt with sensitively, the automatic response could easily convey a flippant attitude. The facial expression and the tone of voice can communicate: "Who cares? Yes, why don't you just get lost and jump ship?"

To prevent mutiny among clients, the business mantra that the customer is always right and is king must be recited again and again. In fact, it would be more advantageous to learn how to sing the mantra. After all, handling objections is part and parcel of being an entrepreneur and in business. What is more, no matter how small and insignificant or humungous the problem is, they all have to be dealt with.

Objections in business are like buildings with subsidence: the longer they are left unattended to, the more a business sinks into a state of disrepair, before eventually having to be brought down in a pile of rubble.

One of the keys to disarming this thief of empowerment is to take the time to find out what everyone's issues are, from staff to customers, including that person who has been labelled one slice short of a loaf. Take the time to confirm the alleged crazy and unreasonable person is what some are saying they are.

Thankfully, handling objections isn't rocket science. Often when a person has the hump the medicine is a listening ear. Many of us have experienced a friend confiding in us when their world has collapsed around them, and after five hours of moaning and a tear or two, weren't you confused when your friend beamed, gave you a hug and said: "Thanks for everything. I just don't know what I would have done without you." The bewildering point is that you didn't do anything apart from nod your head, grunt occasionally and, of course, listen.

Handling objections does not call for an IQ of 140-plus. It's been said that customers' objections are generally their dissatisfactions, which can be satisfied by simply listening and displaying empathy, before attempting to provide a fair solution.

One of the keys to successfully handling business objections is acquiring a strong understanding of people. Once an entrepreneur understands people, business can become a lot easier.

Charles Gordon: "When people ask me if they should study business, I often recommend psychology, instead. With an awareness of how people think, a business person is three-quarters ahead of the game. Psychology teaches you about stereotyping, tunnel vision, the understanding of different behavioural patterns, scapegoating, prejudice; it helps you identify the 'why'."

# Chapter 42

## IT'S NICE TO BE IMPORTANT BUT MORE IMPORTANT TO BE NICE

Charles Gordon: "Wealth can come with its unique type of baggage: arrogance, and being an outright bastard!"

Most of us are familiar with the Golden Rule: "Do to others as you wish them to do to you."

To many, however, the concept of being nice is uncool and simply a blast from a bygone era, particularly in the business arena. If you think of some of the modern-day business magnates--whom I won't name for reasons I'm sure you can understand--few of them are known for their appealing personalities. Instead, the public perception of the powerful is one of a gruff, hard-talking, ruthless individual who made it to the top by stamping on the corns and heads of individuals, when required. In layman's terms, the top man is often portrayed as a real BASTARD!

And so, is there any value in the Golden Rule or living by the principle "It's Nice to be Important, but More Important to be Nice?"

Experience tells us that the way we treat others in life is an investment, one with either high risks and low returns, or high returns that are certain. What I'm trying to say is: how we treat others has an uncanny knack of coming back to bless or haunt us. The Christians would say 'You reap what you sow', while the Buddhists prefer to describe it as karma.

Arrogance and dishonesty comes at a high price. The price can vary from a damaged reputation and becoming a symbolic leper in your community or business field, to doing a stretch (ie, a prison sentence) in Wormwood Scrubs.

The worst-case scenario is to disrespect someone who you completely underestimated, but who in reality is a man of tremendous influence and power: the Boss of Bosses; il Capo di tutti Capi.

For the individual who desires to become empowered, the course of wisdom is to treat everyone equally, by cultivating regal qualities. Yes, we live in an era where manners can be lacking, but those who display qualities such as humility, a genuine interest in others, and grace, will shine brightly and eventually court those with influence.

There are aids in keeping grounded. For those who were reared in impoverished surroundings, a contributing factor is not forgetting back in the day when your diet was minimal--corned beef and rice being the staple diet for a number of days in the week. Or when your plimsolls (this is before the days of trainers) had to be worn with a hole in the sole until sufficient funds were raised.

As you rise to the top in your field of business, you will have to gauge the personality of those around you to clinch business deals and preserve business. The ability to assess the personality of another has been described as the most important skill in acquiring and preserving power. Gaining the insight of another man's personality, however, doesn't come cheap, and requires time and effort as the person in question is researched and observed. It may even require a bit of espionage--007 style!

The British statesman of the 19th century, Lord Chesterfield, is quoted as saying: "Be convinced that there are no persons so insignificant and inconsiderable, but may, some time or other, have it in their power to be of use to you; which they certainly will not, if you have once shown them contempt. Wrongs are often forgiven, but contempt never is. Our pride remembers it for ever."

Charles Gordon: "Be careful what ass you kicked on the way up the financial ladder, because it might be connected to the foot you may have to kiss on your way down."

# Chapter 43

## CUSTOMER SATISFACTION

"Customer satisfaction is about ensuring that everybody who walks out of your exit doors leaves happy. It takes ten minutes to get you a bad reputation, but a lifetime to develop a good one."

Charles Gordon.

Customer satisfaction is a shrewd investment which can cause an entrepreneur to reap kingly treasures.

To enjoy such dividends, a principle that has to be embedded in the heart of any operation is that customers are 'kings' and are always right, even though at times they may be a pain in the butt. After all, without your dear, sweet and at times annoying customers, who will fill your treasure chest? Your business could quickly begin to topple.

Putting up with the oddities of a few clients occasionally, and striving to hit the bullseye in the quality of service is a small sacrifice if the end result will be a thriving business with an impeccable reputation.

Remember that customer satisfaction breeds loyalty and referrals, while customer dissatisfaction results in everything which is cancerous to empowerment--disloyalty, contempt and a determination to advertise just how bad a product or service was provided by this rubbish individual or company. Do you get the picture?

There are no half-measures in customer satisfaction—-it's either sweet or bitter. Empowerment only comes to those who are relentless in trying to maintain a smile on the faces of those who are filling the coffers.

To be able to use customer service to a business's advantage, it's necessary to be aware of the enemies that can rob a company of a high standard of service. These can be many and varied, ranging from a lack of customer knowledge to partiality or slack staff who just don't give a damn.

Training can prevent staff from getting hung up on appearances, since not everyone with a black American Express card wears a twenty-five grand watch. The key to customer satisfaction, and the ensuing benefits, is trying to instil the importance of being fair, honest and just to all customers.

For members of a team who are unable to bow to the king (the customer), references to the Saint Valentines Day Massacre or Hitler's Night of the Long Knives may provide a subtle hint. The only alternative for those who don't meet the high standards of customer satisfaction should be the chop--not literally of course!

# Chapter 44

## BE FIRM BUT FAIR

Maintaining healthy relationships that will help you remain on top as an entrepreneur can be like walking a fine tightrope. Both require a tremendous amount of skill. To prevent a sudden and dramatic fall in one's standing among business colleagues, fine-tuning one's balance is essential.

The challenge that you and every other successful entrepreneur faces is that with power comes the tendency to lose emotional and mental balance. Two qualities that will help you to keep grounded in your dealings with others are firmness and fairness.

Every man or woman at the top has to be firm in their convictions, both to inspire colleagues and ward off prey, who will always be looking for every opportunity to draw blood. Being firm will also prevent chaos spreading from within. For example, can you imagine the effect on an organisation if serious misconduct, be it stealing, fighting or verbal abuse, was tolerated without a firm hand?

On the other hand there are times when a loyal, brilliant colleague may fall short of standards, because of extenuating circumstances; it could be the break up of a marriage, financial difficulties or health concerns. This is when being fair kicks in! To be reasonable in certain circumstances will win the respect of others.

Many may reason that to be fair in business is to ask for their business venture to go six feet under; after all, it's a dog eat dog world. But contrary to popular opinion, to be fair will distinguish you among valuable peers and will result in a number of business advantages. For example, a principled manner of dealing with others will give you conviction, because of awareness that you are both right, and have the best interests of others at heart.

More importantly, being firm and fair will provide added value to your reputation, something which has huge monetary benefits. I'm sure you can recall instances, and it could be many years ago, when a company or individual dealt with you with in a just manner, when it wasn't absolutely necessary, and maybe you can recall how naturally you publicised, for free, the merits of that company or individual!

To have your name and company associated with the two Fs will ultimately lead to another F -- future business -- because of acquiring a fine name. As you become more influential, you will realise that the business scene is a small place and how quickly good or bad deeds spread by word of mouth. The recommendation, therefore, is to always monitor your attitude towards others, by asking the simple question: "Am I being firm, yet fair?"

The principle to take away from 'Be Firm but Fair' is to avoid like the plague the smash-and-grab attitude, which means being unfair and weak. To become powerful you must never forget that it is counter-productive to abuse others.

# Chapter 45

## MY WORD IS MY BOND

"**G**uard your word with your life, because ultimately if your word is not worth shit then you are not worth shit in business."

Charles Gordon

The signature or the fingerprint on the dotted line has formed the basis of millions of business contracts for thousands of years.

Written contracts, however, while essential in any business transaction, are often forged on the premise that 'if you try to play with me or my money I'll sue your arse for every last penny you have'.

When the written contract is coupled with a verbal contract, however, a unique reaction kicks in, resulting in something which is more valuable than money--business ethics, mingled with integrity, trust and friendship.

The motto 'Our Word is our Bond', which can be seen in the heart of the City of London outside the Baltic Exchange, emphasises that the highest level of integrity is essential for traders within that establishment. Those who keep their integrity enjoy unique trading privileges.

The same can be said of entrepreneurs who develop a reputation for living by the principle: "My word is my bond." Such folk will be viewed as noble by those who are like-minded, resulting in them being invited into the inner sanctuaries of the rich and powerful. After all, if you have a lot to protect materially, who would be privy to your dealings? Those who fulfil or those who fluff their vows?

Being half-hearted in living up to your written and verbal contracts will earn an entrepreneur the label 'public enemy number one', for obvious reasons. Broken promises will ultimately result in companies missing deadlines, losing contracts, and of course the loss of valuable income. Never underestimate the damage that can be done to a sparkling reputation by making empty promises. A bad reputation spreads much faster than a good one. A happy client will enthusiastically tell a few about your glorious service, but if they are unhappy God help you because they will tell the world!

The message for any would-be wheeler-dealer is to guard your word with your life, even when this may cause a measure of inconvenience. Remember that what time and energy may be lost because of efforts to complete a task will ultimately be gained in rep as a man or woman of honour. To be endorsed by the right type of person can be worth large sums of money.

Think of this. Each year companies spend millions and millions of pounds on signing up personalities, be it David Beckham or Usain Bolt, to endorse products. They realise that an endorsement from a reputable personality boosts confidence in a product or service, boosting profits. The converse can also be true and is illustrated with Tiger Woods, who lost sponsorship deals with Tag Hauer, Gatorade, and Gillette following allegations of extramarital affairs.

Entrepreneurs can similarly open up opportunities for themselves when the powerful acquire confidence in their talents and reliability. A businessman's loyalty to his word is not a blast from the past. It still boosts business as trust is maintained in relationships, products and services.

# Chapter 46

## AGGRESSION AND ASSERTIVENESS

"The basic difference between being aggressive and being assertive is how our words and behaviour affect the rights and well being of others."
Sharon Anthony

While the difference between aggression and assertiveness is a fine line, the effects caused by the two can be vast: one winning business, while the other squandering potential financial gain.

Let's consider aggression. The warning for the short, insecure type who snarls, points fingers and kicks if need be, is "Beware!" By acquiring a reputation as a boardroom bully the aggressor will undoubtedly leave behind in his wake a trail of hurt and humiliated feelings.

The problem with a businessman who enjoys a good bare-knuckle fight is that he will soon discover that the majority of people are willing and able to use the same tactics. And of course, the problem with every war is that there are casualties, be it in the form of energy, emotions, or more importantly, finance. In short, excessive aggression can be the thick man's tool, in an attempt to get the upper hand.

Assertiveness on the other hand requires far less damage limitation and can boost revenue. There are a number of dynamics, however, that can cause a lack of assertiveness -- for example, a negative self-concept, poor communication skills and a lack of direction in handling conflict situations. A few simple guidelines can help even the ill-experienced entrepreneur to override these negatives.

Being specific in your requests, be it for a larger share of the profits or an earlier delivery date for a product is essential. The manner of communication can also be the difference between being assertive or limp. Those who have mastered the art of being assertive will always make it clear what they are requesting, by using very direct speech. Try it!

What about the scratched record technique? Reminding others by repetition is a powerful tool to build bartering muscle. Imagine concluding a transatlantic deal over the phone and saying, for example: "A million, yes, a million bucks, Mr Trump, yes, I will not go lower than a million dollars."

A more subtle approach can also be helpful for an aspiring entrepreneur to master, in a bid to win others over. This approach works on the premise that if an approach is too forceful then it will cause others to put up a barrier, while subtle suggestions will often cause other to more readily absorb recommendations. According to some estimates, the use of subtle recommendations when initially conducting business has success rates of up to 75 per cent. For the remaining 25 per cent who don't get the point, a more direct or forceful approach can then be used.

Of course, which approach is used will depend on the type of individual or company you are negotiating with, and your objective. For a contractor who is trying to communicate with builders who are late in completing a project, a more forceful approach may be necessary. On the other hand a more persuasive and subtle approach could be necessary during an appointment with a savvy marketing executive.

The bottom line is that everything has to be in moderation. If you acquire a reputation of always being aggressive, others will be desensitised to your approach and eventually will not respond to anything you say. It's all about balance.

How can you detect when you are being an overly aggressive little devil? Think of these questions. Do you interrupt other speakers? Do you display the "I'm always right" syndrome, without taking the time or the decency to listen to others? Do you have the tendency to blame others when you could be in the wrong? If so, chill out!

# Chapter 47

## FAILURE IS NOT AN OPTION

"Success comes to those who become success-conscious. Failure comes to those who indifferently allow themselves to become failure-conscious."
Think and Grow Rich, Napoleon Hill.

For any individual to become success-conscious, programming the subconscious so that one's mind transmits a clear and powerful message that 'failure is not an option' is essential.

The stakes the subconscious plays by are extremely high: all or nothing. Have you noticed that positive and negative emotions cannot occupy the mind at the same time? It is either one or the other.

When planning a business venture, if doubts overwhelm your thoughts of success, you are unlikely to generate the necessary motivation and energy to complete the venture at hand. Negativity and doubts are like yeast: they ferment and quickly consume thinking and stifle positive action.

UK businessman Alexander Amosu made millions after being the first person to produce RnB ringtones for mobile phones in the early 2000s. Yet before hitting the jackpot, he dabbled in a list of enterprises including dance promotion, organising football competitions and running a cleaning company.

The UK entrepreneur is often quoted as saying that it is tenacity and a positive frame of mind which distinguishes the successful person. During an interview at the height of his success he said: "I tried, tried and tried again until I hit gold. There was a niche in the market and luckily I exploited it."

To rise to the challenge of empowering oneself, cultivating the habit of positive thinking is essential. A person must consciously strive to think with hope rather than pessimistically, and courageously rather than in fear.

I have used the words 'strive' and 'cultivate' because it's been said that 90 per cent of the population are trapped in a cycle of negative emotions and actions, believing the lie that they cannot achieve their goals. It is said that only 10 per cent possess a measure of self-belief, which drives them forward to achieve their goals in life.

The distinguished 10 per cent who possess ambition and drive face a problem: avoiding being influenced by the majority who are convinced everyone deserves to experience the same measure of misery as themselves. Am I exaggerating?

Notice the look of contempt you will receive when you reveal to some of the 90 per cent your plans to achieve something noble, or how abruptly the conversation comes to an end, or, worse still, the subtle verbal discouragement that will be levelled at you.

Those who are ensnared in a negative cycle will attempt to dismantle your ideas before they become a reality, and hamstring your confidence before you become a person of note.

To avoid being affected, a person who becomes empowered has to try to surround himself with the mental and spiritual elite: those who acknowledge the power of the subconscious.

Felix Dennis, the owner of Dennis Publishing, the publishers of the magazine Maxim, is said to be worth in the region of £750m. He recently revealed one of his five-point plans to wealth in this way: "Cut loose from nay-sayers and all negative influences. They will tell you about the impossibility of trying to make yourself wealthy. In doing so, they drain confidence from you. They fear that if you should succeed, you will expose their own timidity to the light of day."

When having to associate with those of negative character, avoid be swayed by maintaining your inner independence. In other words, keep yourself from getting emotionally involved, and preserve the unspoken option of being able to leave their company at any moment.

To maintain your inner composure, use what I will refer to as the camouflage ploy. Display the common touch, being all things to men of all sorts, with the goal of blending in to your environment, while avoiding taking sides in the petty squabbles others try to draw you into. By using this ploy you will keep your subconscious refined.

The poet and writer Ella Wheeler Wilcox in her writings demonstrated her understanding of the power of the mind.

In one of her works she wrote:

"You never can tell what your thoughts will do
In bringing you hate or love;
For thoughts are things, and their airy wings
Are swifter than carrier doves.

They follow the law of the universe,
Each thing must create its kind; And they speed o'er the track to bring you back Whatever went out from your mind."

Charles Gordon: "The subconscious is very powerful. If you think you are going to fail, you will. All great achievements begin with a noble thought, seeds that are placed in the imagination, which can grow into realities."

# Chapter 48

## ASSETS AND LIABILITIES

It is a truism to say that to make money is one challenge, but a greater accomplishment is to hold onto the cash that has been earned.

Those who acquire the ability to generate healthy revenue, while spending less, are logically more likely to become and remain empowered. The problem for many is that they find splashing the cash a pleasurable addiction, while saving is far too mundane.

But even when a person becomes a prolific buyer, if he is conscious of the difference between assets and liabilities, his finances can remain robust.

Although this subject covers a vast amount of material, we'll simply define an asset as something that makes money, while a liability loses its purchaser money.

When making substantial purchases, it is beneficial to ask the questions: "Is this item going to be an asset or a liability? Will it make me money, or will I be throwing money down the drain?" The rich often have a knack of looking rich, but spending like a poor man.

The objective of a man or woman of empowerment is to get more assets than liabilities by constantly balancing their books. If £5,000 is blown on liabilities, a successful entrepreneur will acquire the discipline to get £6,000 in assets to recoup losses.

The purchase of a home can potentially be one of the greatest liabilities or assets. If a young, married couple buy a two-bedroom flat in Manchester just before property prices crash in this region, it would of course be a liability.

On the other hand, it would be considered a shrewd move for a single man to buy a two-bedroom flat for rental purposes in Stratford, East London, predicting a hike in property prices because the area will host the Olympics in 2012. His investment would, of course, be viewed as an asset, because of providing an income both for the present and for the long-term.

The difference between those who suffer a liability or enjoy an asset will depend on a variety of factors, such as fluctuations in market value of the product, the buyer's insight into a particular market, and the long-term or short-term perspective of the purchaser.

On some occasions, what a liability or an asset is may not be clear-cut. For example, the purchase of a top-of-the-range Mercedes Benz or a Rolex wristwatch by a young entrepreneur may be viewed as a liability. But the purchase may create the right image during networking, enabling him to make powerful contacts and generate future business. From this perspective, his Mercedes Benz and Rolex watch would be an asset.

A person can begin to have problems with his finances when he becomes a puppet for slick advertising executives, who dictate what to buy and when to buy it--usually the most expensive and now.

Far too many entrepreneurs, particularly those of a younger age, frequently fall prey to the desire for a slick image. They may want to buy top-of-the-range cars, trade from the most prestigious offices, and of course buy the swankiest homes, and it screws up their financial management.

Empowerment is not saying that you should live like Scrooge, but balance is needed. For example, there are certain luxury items that do not lose their value, but can be considered good investments. Classic cars, jewellery made of precious metals, and a Damian Hurst piece of art can earn wise buyers millions of pounds.

Generally, the less spent on liabilities, the more can be invested in making a business more secure in the future, enabling a person to experience his lifestyle ambitions in the future.

A simple equation is that if you have more assets than liabilities then you are heading in the right direction financially.

# Chapter 49

## BULLSHIT BAFFLES THE BRAIN

'Bullshit Baffles the Brain' is a ploy designed to put a spanner in the works during those tense negotiations when a clear head is essential if that all-important deal is to be clinched.

While the title of this chapter may appear odd to some readers, in the business world the concept is frequently used to get a negotiator on the back foot, to scramble brains, to intimidate and to cause the person on the other side of the negotiating table to have an inferiority complex. In short, 'Bullshit Baffles the Brain' can transform a calm, skilled negotiator or investor into a quivering jelly, as if lashed by a Taser electric stun gun.

The devastating effect of bullshit was demonstrated when the biggest fraud in history, involving Bernard Madoff and hedge funds, was uncovered. Reporting on the $50bn skam in December 2008 the Evening Standard newspaper in London wrote: "Throughout the glorious decade just finished, the hedge funds told everybody how brilliant they were. It didn't pay to ask questions, partly because the answers were convoluted but also because their alchemy was a trade secret. Madoff was able to prey on this need for secrecy with devastating effect."

Investors both in England and the US lost millions of and some billions of pounds, because of having their brains baffled.

If a negotiator or investor is to avoid stepping in it, putting at risk the acquisition of a potentially lucrative contract or hard earned cash, it is important to be able to identify a bullshitter. The latter usually speaks in riddles and likes to use long complicated sentences and words, which leaves everyone baffled, even himself!

The bullshitter (B&S) thrives on the unsure and proud who will rarely admit they don't understand the concept being discussed, and so if a person is to avoid being fooled he must be willing to eat humble pie and simply ask: "What the hell are you on about, mate? Can you please translate in layman's terms?"

The experienced businessman who has been confronted by a million and one bullshitters can often see the humorous side of such a character's amateur dramatics and attempts at one-upmanship. When the script is flipped and an explanation is requested regarding the bullshit, a response by way of a blank stare or a garbled sentence can provide a deep feeling of satisfaction.

In short beware of the bullshitter!

# Chapter 50

## MONEY, POWER AND RESPECT

Charles Gordon: "People set money up as a god, but it only provides a person with choices and flexibility. It's important to keep wealth in context."

The person who becomes empowered will be confronted by unique challenges that will attack him on every front. One of the purposes of this

Chapter is to forewarn, so that you can be forearmed to combat the hidden dangers of wealth.

Money, power and respect are what most people crave ahead of happiness and contentment, for a variety of reasons -- possibly because 80 per cent of all banknotes in circulation in England are contaminated with coke and heroin!

On a more serious note, a potential danger for those who acquire wealth was identified by the nobleman Lord Acton, who exclaimed: "Power tends to corrupt; absolute power corrupts absolutely." The challenge the rich man faces is, given the emphasis which is placed on his material assets, will he believe the hype and allow his personality to become a distortion of his true self? With wealth, power and respect there comes a lot of propaganda, which like a circus mirror can cause the head to appear bigger than it should!

For example, those who acquire a measure of wealth will inevitably wield a greater measure of influence over others and may even acquire a measure of respect from others. The reason why I have used the word 'may' is because all too often it is the money that is respected, and not the person. The rich man or woman has a big problem in that few outsiders will see beyond their assets.

The man with money, respect and power has the challenge of maintaining a realistic view of himself and others, despite having to frequently look at himself in a distorted mirror, erected by society. The message is clear: become empowered, yes, but not at the cost of your personality and standards. Occasionally in the pages of Empowerment I have compared the financial systems to a game; call it money go around. Problems start to arise when Mr Bucks takes himself too seriously.

An interesting read on the topic being discussed is the novel American Psycho, by Bret Easton Ellis. The story revolves around an investment banker, Patrick Bateman's, obsession with image and status, which turns him into a serial killer as he strives for recognition from his buddies. Does this mean the dangers of money, power and respect are fiction?

In many parts of London, and other cities a slang word which is frequently used is "diss", meaning to show a lack of respect to another. Within some gang cultures, to diss might involve something as minor as looking at someone in a disapproving manner, to robbing a drugs dealer of his stash. The end result is often violent, all because money, power and respect were violated! The moral of the Chapter is that money, power and respect need to be kept on a leash, by displaying sound values.

Martin Amis in his novel Money wrote: "Money ... It's a fiction, an addiction and a tacit conspiracy."

# Chapter 51

## THE REAL WAY TO START A BUSINESS

There can be a chasm between the real way and the wrong way to start a business. I like to illustrate the difference by comparing two runners on a starting block: one who fails to warm up correctly before the start of the race and yelps in pain after pulling a muscle a few metres down the track, while the other cruises to the finishing line and glory.

The frightening thing about starting a business is that the majority are being taught to fail. I'm not being negative, but realistic. Why else do you think the vast majority of first-time businesses go under within a short time of them starting to trade?

Go to any start-up business seminar or course and, generally speaking, the budding entrepreneur will be told: "Write your business plan, approach your local bank for a loan, start trading and live happily ever after." Right? No, wrong!

Over the years I have observed that aspiring entrepreneurs can be led up the garden path when attending college or some back-street seminar when learning how to start a business. Their experience can fit the description of one of my favourite sayings: "If you take advice from a tramp, you'd better tell him to move over, because you will soon be sitting next to him."

For example, the gullible entrepreneur, having been duped by his lecturer who has never been in business, may be assuming funds will roll in from eager investors, but in reality, what is the likelihood of your financial institution (I don't mean the loan shark), ploughing funds into your fledgling company? I would say almost zero, unless you have a proven track record of business success over many years. In most instances your local bank manger will only lend money on the condition that you cough up half of the loot from your own savings! Just the help you need when you are starting out as an entrepreneur!

And if you are one of the lucky souls who is given a few thousand pounds to start the ball rolling: beware! Starting a business in debt isn't the greatest of foundations on which to build an empire. I would go so far as to say that it could prove to be well dodgy. And who wants to be part-owned by loan sharks anyway? Beware! Trying to jump to the top rung of the ladder can result in severe bruising: loss of home and car, and landing in a pile of debt.

In my experience, the best way to start a business is to start small, with limited overheads and stock in storage. But in reality, every business starting up requires a different formula, depending on the three Ps: price, product and place.

There is no doubt that the internet can prove to be the ideal playing field for the fresh-faced entrepreneur who, with a little research and finance to construct a website, can have access to a global market. In fact, with numerous on-line auction sites such as eBay™ available, the entrepreneur doesn't even have to splash out too much cash before beginning to trade but simply needs a desire to hustle.

Natalie Massenet started an on-line designer shopping website Net-a-Porter, for the 'time poor, cash rich,' in 2000 from a room in Chelsea. The company now employs 300 people in London and New York and is considered to be worth £315m.

## Chapter 52

### MAN MADE THE MONEY AND NOT MONEY THE MAN

Coco Chanel: "There are people who have money and people who are rich."

Even an idiot can understand the logic behind the title of this chapter. Of course coins and notes are made by currency production organisations, such as the Royal Mint and De La Rue. But once money begins to take its toll on the psyche, it has the ability to turn human logic upside down, causing its unknown victims to behave as if money made the man.

The tendency to replace logic with delusions of grandeur is made worse by the messages that are pumped out by society when financial success is achieved.

For example, when a man was broke and driving a Ford Escort he was Mr Invisible and didn't receive a second glance from women. But when you acquire the trappings of success how quickly attitudes change and the former Mr Nobody becomes the most popular man on the block. At times you may get the impression that the vultures can smell money a mile away!

The subtle messages such as: "You're great, numero uno, the business, the man," highlight how people crave and respect money rather than the man. The challenge for you once you become empowered is maintaining your respect for yourself.

Have you noticed how money can cause the most down-to-earth bloke to walk with a swagger, shout rather than request, and turn his nose up at people and situations which previously he would have had a good sniff of.

The danger with adopting the attitude 'Money made the Man' is that the finely-tuned attitude which brought you empowerment can quickly be lost.

Some of the stepping stones to your success which we have discussed at the beginning of this book, such as 'Know Your Worth', 'Being Content' and 'It's Nice to be Important but More Important to be Nice', can be warped if you believe the hype.

And remember the chapter 'Avoid Unhappy and Unlucky' (UUs). If you are to avoid becoming a toxic UU you will need to keep focused on enjoying and being the best at what you do.

Trying to live by the principle that 'Man Made the Money and not Money the Man' against the backdrop of society's propaganda is a tremendous challenge. To maintain your balance will require honest self-evaluation occasionally, and/or the acceptance of straight talking from your buddies.

Charles Gordon: "Don't put so much emphasis on money that it becomes your god. Do not lose sight of your spirituality and balance.

# Chapter 53

## SELF-BELIEF

"The greatest pleasure in life is doing what people say you cannot do."

Walter Bagehot.

To experience the satisfaction of the above statement, self-belief is essential, because there will always be people who are willing to say, "You can't do that."

When the traits of the most powerful and successful people on the planet are considered, self-belief will always be uncovered.

Muhammad Ali became the greatest boxer in history because of his self-belief. What else helped him to accurately predict the round he would put his opponents on the canvas?

But I hear you saying to yourself: "That was boxing, not business."

But the same belief which is required to knock a man down in the boxing ring can also be used to be in the boardroom.

The problem is that self-belief is a rare commodity today. I'm sure we all have friends or family members who possess a well of brilliant ideas which if implemented would earn them enough money to retire at a young age. But, like many people, when they are asked enthusiastically: "How is your project developing?" their response is one timid excuse after another. While such responses may be confusing, the facial expression often reveals the main issue, a lack of self-belief.

The drought of self-belief in this world shouldn't be a surprise. Have you noticed how rare it is find individuals who have any belief in your ability and potential? In fact, have you noticed the frequency of persons, including teachers, who take great delight in draining the confidence and drive from young, impressionable minds?

How many times have we been told the anecdote involving the enthusiastic young pupil who wants to become a lawyer, a politician or a premiership footballer and approaches his careers teacher for advice? Unfortunately for him, he approached a person whose confidence in life was shattered 30 years ago and who finds joy in doing the same to others.

The response given to the young pupil can range from a subtle "I think managing a local Kentucky Fried Chicken shop will be more suitable for you" type answer, to a straight "Get out of here!" or a rare "I'm going to help you reach your goal."

To nurture your self-belief, look for ways to condition your mind to believe that you can, to counteract the propaganda that surrounds you. Alexander the Great was surrounded by parents and teachers who conditioned him to believe that he was destined for greatness.

The more you know yourself and understand your motivations, and your unique mix of talents and abilities, the greater will be your self-belief.

Successful entrepreneurs tend to focus on projects which identify that spark of magic or the divine within themselves, which distinguishes them from the average.

Bill Gates is very, very rich because he believed in himself. He clung to Microsoft stock when experts were saying they were at their peak, because he believed that what he was doing would become more successful each year. In 1987, at the age of 31 he became the youngest billionaire ever.

It's been said that everyone is born unique but most of us die copies. To become empowered, strive to be unique.

# Chapter 54

## BEING CONTENT

"**A** mere lover of silver will not be satisfied with silver, neither any lover of wealth with income."

Solomon, Ecclesiastes 5:10.

Contentment is a double-edged sword. A lack of it can provide the motivation to rise above disadvantage and adversity, while also having the potential to break a person once he has 'made it', if there is not balance.

Too much of the C-substance, on the other hand, can cause a person to languish in a state of inactivity, like a curled-up pussy next to a fire.

While a balanced measure of contentment is essential to a healthy mental and emotional state, few attain it, not even the wealthy, noble or so-called 'great'.

Alexander the Great didn't possess contentment and his lust for ambition drove him to keep conquering nations until his vitality was entirely depleted. Today we would call it burnout! It is rumoured that eventually he died from the bite of a mosquito!

The moral of the story is beware--money, power and success can be very addictive, particularly for empty heads. To illustrate the point I am making, a few years ago a neighbour asked me to look after his flat while he went on holiday. One of the tasks I was given was to feed his beloved goldfish. The only problem was, I became a bit heavy-handed when dishing out the fishy food and instead of placing one flake on the surface of the water, supplied them with a week's food in one session, by mistake.

Because fish are empty-headed, they will eat and eat and eat and eat! They have no concept of being content. As long as the food is available, fish will consume it until they implode, which is exactly what happened. Needless to say, my neighbour never allowed me to look after his fish again when going away on holiday.

Sad to say, many in business do not know when to say 'enough is enough', bringing tremendous problems on themselves--ranging from health to family issues and addictions to various mind-altering substances.

Part of the problem for entrepreneurs is the measuring line for success in business is not as clean-cut as in the professions and is frequently assessed simply by wealth; hence the reason why many spend their whole lives chasing money.

The contentment void has another trap. Those who crave money, success and power, yet taste little of it, can often resort to desperate measures to earn money.

To avoid the snares of a lack of contentment, recognise that worthwhile achievements take time to become a reality. Qualities have to be developed, plans put in train and action fostered.

A person who wants to achieve genuine empowerment sets reasonable goals to maintain a measure of momentum in life, which has the effect of staving off the nagging feeling of a lack of contentment in the process.

With contentment comes an aura of power that can open doors of opportunity. We have all been confronted by the individual who is desperate for money, sex and status, and we try to run a mile when we smell them coming. But the content have an air of wealth, refreshment and strength which attracts attention. It is then up to each individual to use the attention received to his or her benefit.

# Chapter 55

## THE CON ENDS HERE

So, you've reached the con-clusion, have you?!

I hope reading the pages of Empowerment hasn't been a theoretical exercise causing you to find a convenient excuse to slip this book under the bed or onto the bookshelf where it will simply gather dust and you will forget what you have been taught.

All too often an unfulfilled life is riddled can be riddled with lame excuses that are wheeled out when an individual just doesn't have the bottle to go for it in life!

Have you noticed how many would-be entrepreneurs have 50,000 different reasons why they can't achieve this and can't achieve that? The reality is, if they spent the same amount of time focusing on how they can achieve, their life would be far more rewarding. The 55 Laws of Empowerment are the secrets which the elite use to stay on top and so why not use them yourself?

One of the chapters in this book is entitled 'Avoid Unhappy and Unlucky', because of their ability to drain the energy, charisma, self-esteem and creativity of any sucker they can get their fangs into. I would add to that statement: avoid excuses and those who have the habit of making them –– it can be infectious.

One of my frequently used quotations that reflects my disdain of a lazy mindset is: "Excuses are like assholes: everyone has them and they stink." Please, don't think I'm crude or need counselling for anger management, but I'm convinced excuses are like a modern-day plague which causes mass paralysis.

In the Preface to this book, the appeal was to the type of person who enjoys the thrill and challenge of thinking and living outside the figurative box, and so I'm guessing that, unlike the personality type mentioned in this chapter, you are the type of person who, on sensing a good thing, likes to get the bit between their teeth. My advice, however, is: not too quickly and not all at once, you might choke!

The principles laid out in the Secrets of Empowerment are rich pickings which may take a little time to digest. I also describe them as instruments of magic, which provide the props and set the scene on the stage for performing in the business world. The advice from the old head is: don't feel too disappointed if, at your first few attempts at enterprise, you fail to perform like a modern-day Houdini and dazzle your potential business partners with your tricks, causing them to concede to your every whim! Remember you are on a learning curve, but with practice, practice and more practice on how to use the instruments of magic you can become a master and beat the system at its own game.

Remember the chapter 'Long-Term Strategy'? The encouragement was to be one step ahead of your competitors by understanding what makes them tick mentally. Closely linked to the ability to strategise is 'Choosing Your Battles', another key to Empowerment. Generally, the man of power has the knack of identifying the sources and opportunities which will recharge or replenish his reputation and financial status. The novice, on the other hand, often adopts an 'all-guns-blazing' approach to business opportunities, which can result in him getting bogged down in different ventures that do little to bolster his wealth. Avoid trench warfare!

What you'll discover is that your ability to come up the ranks has much to do with 'Concealing Your Intentions', so that you are not viewed as a threat. Never forget that most men will always want to stay in power, even if they only have a few more years to live. An overtly ambitious man is often viewed as Public Enemy Number One and targeted for a premature fall from grace. Use your head and 'Always Express Mutual Benefits'. The successful entrepreneur often fools the man at the top by wisely giving the impression that he is appealing to the self-interest of his potential investors, rather than himself.

The majority of what I have written hopefully appeals to logic, which is what successful business is often about. The purpose of this is to reinforce the notion that successful entrepreneurs are not born but are created, often from a variety of circumstances and acquired qualities, such as conviction, confidence and effective communication.

But even with the best will in the world: without a strategy, it ain't happening. And so, from today, why not write down your strategy: what you have to do and what you want to do. You will be surprised at what you will eventually achieve in the realms of 'Money, Power and Respect.' Thinking of that chapter, don't take yourself too seriously, since Man Made the Money, Not Money Made the Man. And remember, "Yes You Can."